CUTE
CREATURES
TO KNIT AND CROCHET

Search Press

CUTE CREATURES

TO KNIT AND CROCHET

Éditions MARIE CLAIRE :
Head of publishing : Thierry Lamarre
Editorial clerk : Adeline Lobut
Design and production : Charlotte Rion
Creation : Marie Noelle Bayard
Photographs : Pierre Nicou
Retoucher/digital operator : Jean-Michel Boillot
Explanations : Renée Méry
Diagrams and grids : Olivier Ribaillier
Editorial office : Véronique Blanc
Artistic direction, layout : Either Studio

Contents

DISCOVERING CUTE CREATURES   P . 0 8

PLAYFUL PUPPETS   P . 1 6

FRIENDLY CREATURES   P . 2 6

WACKY CREATURES   P . 4 2

CROCHETED ANIMAL CHARMS   P . 5 2

INSTRUCTIONS   P . 6 2

Index

DISCOVERING CUTE CREATURES

Made from French knitting applied to fabric, these lively creatures make perfect little gifts.

Big mouse .... **p. 10**
Little mouse .... **p. 11**
Big dog .... **p. 12**
Little dog .... **p. 13**
Owl .... **p. 14**
Tortoise .... **p. 15**

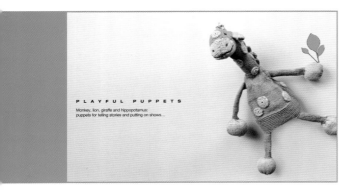

PLAYFUL PUPPETS

Monkey, lion, giraffe and hippopotamus: puppets for telling stories and putting on shows...

Monkey .... **p. 18**
Lion .... **p. 20**
Giraffe .... **p. 22**
Hippopotamus .... **p. 24**

FRIENDLY CREATURES

Zebras, bears, penguins, dogs and cats...
cute, friendly animals for cuddling...

Polar bear .... p. 28
Black bear .... p. 30
Mother penguin .... p. 32
Baby penguins .... p. 33
Zebra .... p. 34
Fat cat .... p. 36
Yin yang dogs .... p. 38
Cuddly cat .... p. 40

WACKY CREATURES

These multi-coloured, surprising, wacky animals
have been 'redesigned' just for fun...

Fanfan the elephant .... **p. 44**
Antoinette the little hen .... **p. 46**
Felix the Martian dog .... **p. 48**
Big wolf, little wolf .... **p. 50**

CROCHETED ANIMAL CHARMS

Fashionable, cute little amigurumi-style animals to attach to
your bag, purse or key ring. Just as popular with adults as with
children, these charming animals are quick to make.

Dachshund .... p. 54
Chihuahua .... p. 55
Hedgehog .... p. 56
Squirrel .... p. 57
Sheep .... p. 58
Pig and cow .... p. 59
Bear .... p. 60
Donkey and frog .... p. 61

DISCOVERING CUTE CREATURES

Made from French knitting applied to fabric, these lively creatures make perfect little gifts.

1

BIG MOUSE

Spiral a length of French knitting on to the fabric base, attach the felt nose and ears, embroider the eyes and you have a great mouse toy – simple.
Created in DK (sport) weight yarn (50% wool/50% acrylic) with nose and ears in felt or polar fleece.
Instructions on page 66.

2 LITTLE MOUSE

Made in the same way as its larger companion but in a different colour, this little mouse is so adorable that you could easily build up a whole family.

Created in DK (sport) weight yarn (50% wool/50% acrylic) with nose and ears in felt or polar fleece.
Instructions on page 67.

3 BIG DOG

This cute creature is made by spiralling French knitting over a fabric base, with a contrasting colour for the ears. It's as easy as it is fun.
Created in DK (sport) weight yarn (100% cotton) with a felt or polar fleece nose and feet and embroidered features.
Instructions on page 68.

LITTLE DOG

This small dog is made in the reverse colours to his larger companion, with an orange body and white ears this time.
Created in DK (sport) weight yarn (100% cotton) with a felt or polar fleece nose and feet and embroidered features.
Instructions on page 69.

EASY

5 OWL

With his poached-egg eyes and bewildered expression, this fat little owl has loads of character.
Created in DK (sport) weight yarn (100% cotton) and DK (sport) weight yarn (50% wool/50%
acrylic) with a felt or polar fleece beak, eyes and feet.
Instructions on page 70.

EASY

EASY

6

TORTOISE

This tortoise loves leftovers so make him from colourful fabric scraps and yarns.
Created in DK (sport) weight yarn (50% wool/50% acrylic) and 4-ply (fingering) weight yarn
(30% lambswool/70% acrylic) with multi-coloured felt or polar-fleece limbs.
Instructions on page 71.

PLAYFUL PUPPETS

Monkey, lion, giraffe and hippopotamus:
puppets for telling stories and putting on shows…

7

MONKEY

This young lady monkey wears a pretty pink frock with a chevron edging.
Make the dress in your child's favourite colours.
Knitted in DK (sport) weight yarn (50% wool/50% acrylic) and DK (sport) weight yarn (25% wool/25% acrylic/50% polyamide) using 2.5mm (US size 1) knitting needles.
Instructions on page 72.

8 LION

A brilliant yellow mane made from polar fleece adds character to this fine lion puppet.
Knitted in DK (sport) weight yarn (50% wool/50% acrylic) using 2.5mm (US size 1) knitting needles.
Instructions on page 75.

9 GIRAFFE

Simple crocheted spots and horns add character to this colourful knitted giraffe puppet; garter stitch on the lower edge of the costume adds further texture.
Knitted in merino DK (sport) weight wool yarn and
4-ply (fingering) weight yarn (30% lambswool/70% acrylic)
using 3mm (US size 3) knitting needles and a 2.5mm
(US size 1/C) crochet hook.
Instructions on page 78.

10

HIPPOPOTAMUS

This colourful knitted cutie has a handy front pocket, which you could use for an additional little gift. Knitted in 4-ply (fingering) weight yarn (30% lambswool/70% acrylic) using 2.5mm (US size 1) knitting needles.
Instructions on page 81.

FRIENDLY CREATURE

Zebras, bears, penguins, dogs and cats…
cute, friendly animals for cuddling…

POLAR BEAR

A fluffy yarn ensures that this sweet little bear will never run short of cuddles.
Knitted in soft textured DK (sport) weight yarn (100% polyester) and DK (sport) weight yarn
(25% wool/25% acrylic/ 50% polyamide) with 2.5cm (US size 1) and 3mm (US size 3) knitting needles.
Instructions on page 83.

BLACK BEAR

This cartoonlike black-and-white bear has a knitted body with crocheted eyes and tummy. The limbs are thread-jointed so they articulate.
Knitted and crocheted in DK (sport) weight yarn (25% wool/25% acrylic/ 50% polyamide) with 2.5mm (US size 1) knitting needles and a 2.5mm (US size 1/C) crochet hook.
Instructions on page 85.

MOTHER PENGUIN

With her chubby body, bright yellow bill and orange feet, this super penguin is a delight. She has a moss-stitch back and wings for added texture.
Knitted in DK (sport) weight yarn (100% cotton) with 2.5mm (US size 1) knitting needles.
Instructions on page 88.

14, 15

BABY PENGUINS

Knitted in the same way as their mother, but with simpler feet, these cuties are a lot of fun and their small size makes them quick to make.
Knitted in DK (sport) weight yarn (100% cotton) with 2.5mm (US size 1) knitting needles.
Instructions on page 90.

16

ZEBRA

One of the easiest projects in this book, this zippy zebra is made from rectangles of knitting, stuffed and stitched together.
Knitted in DK (sport) weight yarn (50% wool/50% acrylic) with 2.5mm (US size 1) knitting needles.
Instructions on page 92.

FAT CAT

With his slightly startled expression and fluffy body, tail and ears, this fat cat will always produce a smile.
Knitted in soft textured chunky 100% polyester yarn and DK (sport) weight yarn (25% wool/25% acrylic/ 50% polyamide) with 3mm (US size 3) and 4.5mm (US size 7) knitting needles, with a tail crocheted using a 5mm (US size H) crochet hook.
Instructions on page 94.

YIN YANG DOGS

These stylized dogs are packed with personality. Knitted in stocking stitch, they each have a crocheted eye patch in the opposite colour, yin yang style.
Made in DK (sport) weight yarn (100% cotton) using 2.5mm (US size 1) knitting needles and a 2.5mm (US size 1/C) crochet hook.
Instructions on pages 95 and 96.

20

CUDDLY CAT

Made with the head and body combined, this long-limbed cat is surprisingly quick and easy to knit. His tail is worked in basic crochet.
Knitted in soft, elastic baby yarn and DK (sport) weight yarn (25% wool/25% acrylic/50% polyamide) using 3mm (US size 3) and 5mm (US size 8) knitting needles and a 4mm (US size G) crochet hook.
Instructions on page 98.

WACKY CREATURES

These multi-coloured, surprising, wacky animals
have been 'redesigned' just for fun…

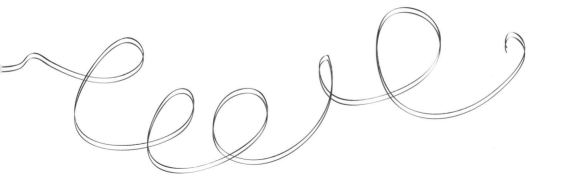

FANFAN THE ELEPHANT

This eccentric elephant, knitted in stocking stitch and garter stitch, is made in four colours. Take the opportunity to use up yarn left over from other projects – you could even add more colours. Knitted in DK (sport) weight yarn (50% wool/50% acrylic) and 4-ply (fingering) weight yarn (30% lambswool/70% acrylic) using 3mm (US size 3) and 4mm (US size 6) knitting needles. Instructions on page 99.

22

ANTOINETTE THE LITTLE HEN

With her multi-layered skirt and jaunty comb this funky chicken is ready to party.
Her beak and eyes are made from felt or polar fleece.
Knitted in DK (sport) weight yarn (100% cotton) using 2.5mm (US size 1) knitting needles.
Instructions on page 101.

FELIX THE MARTIAN DOG

With its bold colours, large felt eyes, crazy antennae and scarf, this dog is truly out of this world. The garter-stitch body is quick to make and the striped sections are a lot of fun.
Knitted in DK (sport) weight yarn (25% wool/40% acrylic/35% chlorofibre) using 2.5mm (US size 1) and 5mm (US size 8) knitting needles.
Instructions on page 103.

24, 25

BIG WOLF, LITTLE WOLF

These stylized wolves would make great gifts for brothers or sisters. They are made with plain and striped stocking stitch with felt or polar fleece eyes.

Knitted in DK (sport) weight yarn (50% wool/50% acrylic) using 2.5mm (US size 1) knitting needles.

Instructions on page 104 and 107.

CROCHETED ANIMAL CHARMS

Fashionable, cute little amigurumi-style animals to attach to your bag, purse or key ring. Just as popular with adults as with children, these charming animals are quick to make.

26
DACHSHUND

With his floppy ears, perky tail and cute embroidered nose you can't help but love this happy pup. Crocheted in DK (sport) weight yarn (50% wool/50% acrylic) using a 1.75mm (US size 6) crochet hook and incorporating a swivel snap hook. Instructions on page 109.

27

CHIHUAHUA

This delightful chihuahua has a separate muzzle and eyes to give his face added dimension;
his eyes and nose are embroidered.
Crocheted in DK (sport) weight yarn (50% wool/50% acrylic) using a 1.75mm (US size 6) crochet
hook and incorporating a swivel snap hook.
Instructions on page 110.

28

HEDGEHOG

Made in just six pieces, this little guy has spines that are easily made by attaching lengths of yarn with a crochet hook.

Crocheted in DK (sport) weight yarn (50% wool/50% acrylic) using a 1.75mm (US size 6) crochet hook and incorporating a swivel snap hook.

Instructions on page 112.

29

SQUIRREL

This perky squirrel's amazing tail is created using a novelty yarn.
Crocheted in 4-ply (fingering) weight yarn (30% lambswool/70% acrylic), DK (sport) weight yarn
(50% wool/50% acrylic) and Aran (worsted) weight eyelash yarn using 1.75mm (US size 6) and
2mm (US size 4) crochet hooks and incorporating a swivel snap hook.
Instructions on page 114.

30

SHEEP

This little sheep has a pink face and ears and simple embroidered features.
Crocheted in DK (sport) weight yarn (50% wool/50% acrylic) using a 1.75mm (US size 6) crochet
hook and incorporating a swivel snap hook.
Instructions on page 116.

31

PIG

Made in just one colour, with French knots for eyes, this charming little pig has a long snout, cute triangular ears and a little tail – for pig lovers everywhere.
Crocheted in DK (sport) weight yarn (50% wool/50% acrylic) using a 1.75mm (US size 6) crochet hook and incorporating a swivel snap hook.
Instructions on page 118.

32

COW

This brindled cow is easier to make than you might think because her markings are added with embroidery.
Crocheted in DK (sport) weight yarn (50% wool/50% acrylic) using a 1.75mm (US size 6) crochet hook and incorporating a swivel snap hook.
Instructions on page 120.

33

BEAR

Made in two shades of brown with a vibrant orange nose, this little bear is easy and fun to make. Crocheted in DK (sport) weight yarn (50% wool/50% acrylic) and 4-ply (fingering) weight yarn (30% lambswool/70% acrylic) using a 1.75mm (US size 6) crochet hook and incorporating a swivel snap hook.
Instructions on page 122.

34

DONKEY

This wonderful character has clever two-colour ears and a contrasting muzzle. His features are embroidered.
Crocheted in DK (sport) weight yarn (50% wool/50% acrylic) using a 1.75mm (US size 6) crochet hook and incorporating a swivel snap hook. Instructions on page 124.

35

FROG

Embroidered orange eyes and a big grin bring this little fellow to life. The eyes and mouth are made separately for added dimension.
Crocheted in DK (sport) weight yarn (50% wool/50% acrylic) and 4-ply (fingering) weight yarn (30% lambswool/70% acrylic) using a 1.75mm (US size 6) crochet hook and incorporating a swivel snap hook. Instructions on page 126.

INSTRUCTIONS

 **DISCOVERING CUTE CREATURES** **PLAYFUL PUPPETS** **FRIENDLY CREATURES** **WACKY CREATURES** **CROCHETED ANIMAL CHARMS**

ASSEMBLING THE PIECES

The pieces that make up the animals can be sewn together in different ways depending on their size, how they are placed on the animal and your level of skill.

Use the most suitable sewing method. Larger pieces can be joined with right sides facing and then turned right sides out to hide the seams before stuffing. If preferred, the pieces can be joined with right sides out and then filled immediately. In both instances, the opening is sewn up from the right side.

Using marks. Marks on the patterns make it easier to put together more complex cuddly toys. Pin the pieces together, matching up the marks, and then follow the instructions with each project.

Lining. All the animals are knitted fairly tightly but to be extra safe and secure, it is possible to line them. To cut the lining pieces, place the ironed knitted sections on to some cotton fabric. Cut around each piece, adding 0.5cm (¼in) for the seams, then make up the fabric animal in the same way as the knitted one, sliding each fabric shape into the corresponding knitted shape before sewing together. This way it will be impossible to pull out the filling from between the knitted stitches.

THE STITCHES
KNIT STITCHES
Garter stitch: Knit every row.
Stocking stitch: Knit every right-side row; purl every wrong-side row.
Moss stitch (even number of stitches):
Row 1: *knit 1, purl 1*; repeat from * to * to the end.
Row 2: *purl 1, knit 1*; repeat from * to * to the end.
CROCHET STITCHES
In each project, the US crochet terms are given first, followed by the UK terms in brackets.
Foundation chain and chain stitch (ch): Starting with a slipknot, wrap the yarn over the hook and draw it through the loop; repeat as required.
Slip stitch (sl st): Insert the hook into the work as instructed, wrap the yarn over the hook then draw the yarn through in one movement.

US single crochet (sc)/**UK double crochet** (dc): Insert hook into stitch as instructed, wrap yarn over hook and draw yarn through work. Wrap yarn over hook, draw yarn through both loops on hook.
US reversed single crochet/UK reversed double crochet: Like double crochet stitches, but worked from left to right.
US half double crochet (hdc)/**UK half treble** (htr): Wrap yarn over hook and insert hook into stitch as instructed. Yarn over again and draw through work (three loops on hook), yarn over again and draw through all three loops on hook.
US double crochet (dc)/**UK treble** (tr): Wrap yarn over hook and insert hook into stitch as instructed. Yarn over hook, draw through work (three loops on hook), yarn over hook again and draw through first two loops (two loops on hook), yarn over hook and draw through last two loops.

FRENCH KNITTING

All the animals made from French knitting are created following the same steps. For this you will need a French knitter (also known as a 'dolly').

1 Make the length(s) of French knitting as instructed for each project. To finish off the French knitting, first thread the yarn through a large needle. Thread it through the four stitches and pull up the thread; knot the thread and hide the end inside the tube of French knitting.

2 Reproduce the patterns (by enlarging them on a photocopier if necessary as explained below). Cut them out of the fabric according to the number required, adding 1cm (½in) all around for the seams. (Polar fleece and felt pieces do not require a seam allowance because they do not fray so cut them to the same size as the pattern.)

3 Make the animals in fabric then stuff them.

4 Cover the fabric animals with the French knitting, as explained below, firmly attaching it in place.

5 Add the detailing: eyes, beak, mouth, etc. in felt/polar fleece or with embroidery.

ENLARGING THE PATTERNS

Each pattern comes with a 5cm (2in) measurement line. Start by calculating the enlargement percentage so that this line will actually measure 5cm (2in). To do this, first measure the line for the animal you wish to make and divide 5 by your answer. For example, if the line measures 1.5cm, then make the following calculation: $5 \div 1.5 = 3.33$. Now multiply by 100. The percentage enlargement must be 333%. First enlarge by 200%, the maximum level for photocopiers. For the second enlargement, perform the following calculation: $333 \div 200 = 1.66$. The percentage for the second enlargement is 166%. If the result of the first calculation is lower than 2, set the photocopier straight to this percentage.

MAKING THE ANIMALS

Place the pieces of cloth right sides together and, using backstitch or a sewing machine, sew along the line leaving an opening large enough to turn the fabric through. Cut notches into the seam allowances at the curves. If necessary, adjust the notches to give maximum flexibility. Turn out and fill. Close the opening.

ATTACHING THE CORDS OF FRENCH KNITTING

Pin the French knitting in a spiral over the fabric, working with small sections at a time. Attach it to the fabric with strong thread in matching colours, as required, using slip stitch through the fabric and the edge of the French knitting, so that the stitches are hidden by the next row of French knitting. Slip the final end under the previous row, at an angle, and stitch in place.

DISCOVERING CUTE CREATURES

PLAYFUL PUPPETS

FRIENDLY CREATURES

WACKY CREATURES

CROCHETED ANIMAL CHARMS

1 BIG MOUSE

SIZE: about 12cm (4¾in) long

MATERIALS

DK (sport) weight yarn (50% wool/50% acrylic): 1 ball of deep pink
Cotton fabric in ecru
Scrap of deep pink felt or polar fleece for the ears
Scrap of grey felt or polar fleece for the nose
French knitter
Light grey embroidery thread/yarn
Synthetic filling
Deep pink and grey sewing threads

INSTRUCTIONS

Make around 3.5m (4yd) of French knitting.
From cotton fabric: cut two sides and one base, adding 1cm (½in) all around for seams.
From deep pink felt/polar fleece: cut two ears.
From grey felt/polar fleece: cut one triangle for the nose.

1 Sew together the two cotton side pieces along the curved back seam; attach to the base, matching up the centres with the ends of the back seam (see page 65). Turn out, stuff and close the gap.
2 Pin one end of the French knitting to the end of the nose and wind it over the whole mouse, stitching the French knitting in place as you go. Finish in the centre at the rear of the mouse. Leave 30cm (12in) of French knitting hanging for the tail. Cut and finish off. Tie a knot in the end of the tail.
3 Sew the nose in place using grey thread.
4 Slip the base of the ears between two rows of French knitting and sew them on securely.
5 Work a little French knot in light grey embroidery thread/yarn to mark each eye.

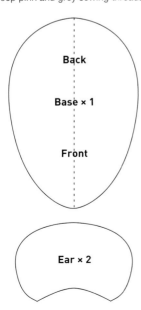

Back

Base × 1

Front

Ear × 2

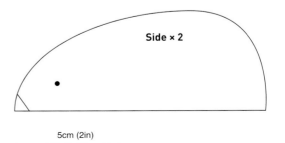

Side × 2

5cm (2in)

2 LITTLE MOUSE

SIZE: about 10cm (4in) long

MATERIALS

DK (sport) weight yarn (50% wool/50% acrylic): 1 ball of light grey
Cotton fabric in ecru
Scraps of deep pink felt or polar fleece for the nose and ears
Black embroidery thread/yarn
French knitter
Synthetic filling
Matching sewing threads

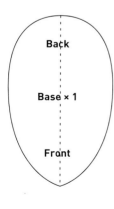

Back

Base × 1

Front

Ear × 2

INSTRUCTIONS

Make around 2m (2yd) of French knitting.
From cotton fabric: cut two sides and one base, adding 1cm (½in) all around for seams.
From felt/polar fleece: cut one triangle for the nose and two ears.

1 Sew together the two cotton side pieces along the curved back seam; attach to the base, matching up the centres with the ends of the back seam (see page 65). Turn out, stuff and close the gap.
2 Pin one end of the French knitting to the end of the nose and wind it over the whole mouse, stitching the French knitting in place as you go. Finish in the centre at the rear of the mouse. Leave 25cm (10in) of French knitting hanging for the tail. Cut and finish off. Tie a knot in the end of the tail.
3 Sew the nose in place.
4 Slip the base of the ears between two rows of French knitting and sew them on securely.
5 Work a little French knot in black embroidery thread/yarn to mark each eye.

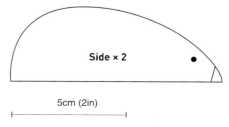

Side × 2

5cm (2in)

DISCOVERING CUTE CREATURES

PLAYFUL PUPPETS

FRIENDLY CREATURES

WACKY CREATURES

CROCHETED ANIMAL CHARMS

3 BIG DOG

SIZE: about 10cm (4in) high and wide

MATERIALS

DK (sport) weight yarn (100% cotton): 1 ball each of white (**A**) and orange (**B**)
Two 10cm (4in) squares of cotton fabric in ecru
Scraps of orange felt or polar fleece for the nose, paws and ears
French knitter
Synthetic filling
Orange and white sewing threads

INSTRUCTIONS

Make around 4.5m (5yd) of French knitting in **A** and 1.5m (1½yd) of French knitting in **B**.
From cotton fabric: cut two body pieces, adding 1cm (½in) all around for seams.
From felt/polar fleece: cut two feet, two ears and one muzzle (use the pattern or simply cut a circle).

1 Sew the body pieces together around the edges, leaving a gap to turn through. Turn out, stuff and close the gap (see page 65).
2 Pin 3cm (1¼in) of one end of the French knitting in **A** vertically to the centre of the front and cover the whole of the front, winding it in a spiral and stitching as you go. Carry on across the back, ending in the centre. Leave 30cm (12in) of French knitting hanging for the tail. Cut and finish off. Tie a knot in the end of the tail.
3 Cover each ear in the same way using French knitting in **B**, starting at the centre and slipping the final end under the previous row.
4 Sew an ear at the top of each side of the body.
5 Attach the muzzle using large running stitches in **A**. Embroider the nose at the centre in satin stitch using **A**; embroider the eyes in satin stitch using **B**.
6 Attach the feet underneath the body using backstitch along the straight edge.

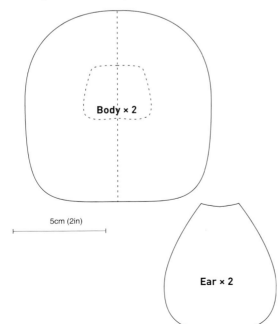

Body × 2

5cm (2in)

Ear × 2

Foot × 2

4 LITTLE DOG

SIZE: about 8cm (3in) high and wide

MATERIALS

DK (sport) weight yarn (100% cotton): 1 ball each of orange (**A**) and white (**B**)
Two 12 × 14cm (4¾ × 5½in) cotton fabric rectangles in ecru
Scraps of white felt or polar fleece for the nose, paws and ears
French knitter
Synthetic filling
Orange and white sewing threads

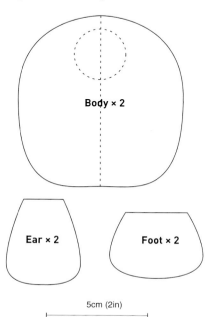

Body × 2

Ear × 2

Foot × 2

5cm (2in)

INSTRUCTIONS

Make around 3m (3¼yd) of French knitting in **A** and 1m (1yd) of French knitting in **B**.
From cotton fabric: cut two body pieces, adding 1cm (½in) all around for seams.
From felt/polar fleece: cut two feet, two ears and one circle for the muzzle.

1   Sew the body pieces together around the edges, leaving a gap to turn through. Turn out, stuff and close the gap (see page 65).
2   Pin one end of the French knitting in **A** to the centre of the front and cover the whole of the front, winding it in a spiral and stitching as you go. Carry on across the back, ending in the centre. Leave 15cm (6in) of French knitting hanging for the tail. Cut and finish off. Tie a knot in the end of the tail.
3   Cover each ear in the same way using French knitting in **B**, starting at the centre and slipping the final end under the previous row.
4   Sew an ear at the top of each side of the body.
5   Attach the muzzle using large running stitches in **A**. Embroider the nose in satin stitch in the centre using **A**; embroider the eyes in satin stitch using **B**.
6   Attach the feet underneath the body using backstitch along the straight edge.

5 OWL

SIZE: about 10cm (4in) high

MATERIALS

DK (sport) weight yarn (100% cotton): 1 ball of purple (**A**)
DK (sport) weight yarn (50% wool/50% acrylic): 1 ball of deep pink (**B**)
Cotton fabric in ecru
Scraps of felt or polar fleece: deep pink for the wings, orange for the feet, yellow for the beak and white for the eyes
French knitter
Orange and light green embroidery thread/yarn
Synthetic filling
Matching sewing threads

INSTRUCTIONS

Make around 4m (4½yd) of French knitting in **A** and 1m (1yd) of French knitting in **B**.
From cotton fabric: cut four body pieces, adding 1cm (½in) all around for seams.
From felt/polar fleece: cut two deep pink wings, two orange feet, two oval white eyes and a yellow triangle for the beak.

1 Sew two body pieces together for the back along the curved centre-back seam; repeat for the front. Sew the side seams, leaving a gap to turn through; turn out, stuff and close the gap (see page 65).

2 Pin one end of the French knitting in **A** to the centre of the stomach, then cover the whole of the body, winding it in a spiral and stitching as you go. Carry on across the back, ending in the centre.

3 Cover the wings in the same way using French knitting in **B**. Sew the top of one wing to each side of the body at the head end.

4 Sew the beak in place using backstitch in orange embroidery thread/yarn, parallel to the edges. Sew the eyes above using running stitch in light green. Embroider the pupils with satin stitch in orange.

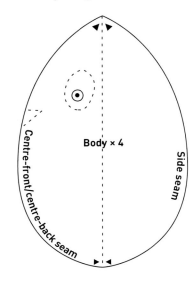

Body × 4

Centre-front/centre-back seam

Side seam

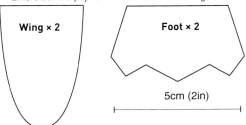

Wing × 2

Foot × 2

5cm (2in)

5 Attach the feet underneath the body using backstitch along the straight edge.

6 TORTOISE

SIZE: about 10cm (4in) long

MATERIALS

DK (sport) weight yarn (50% wool/50% acrylic: 1 ball of pale green (**A**)
4-ply (fingering) weight yarn (30% lambswool/70% acrylic): 1 ball of mid green (**B**)
Cotton fabric in ecru
Scraps of felt and/or polar fleece in turquoise, green, orange, red, mint green and sky blue
Pink embroidery thread/yarn
French knitter
Synthetic filling
Matching sewing threads

INSTRUCTIONS

Make around 2.5m (2¾yd) of French knitting in A and 1.8m (2yd) of French knitting in B.
From cotton fabric: cut two backs and one base, adding 1cm (½in) all around for seams.
From felt/polar fleece: cut two turquoise heads and eight legs in mixed colours, adding 0.5cm (¼in) all around for seams.

1. Sew the two back pieces together along the rounded centre-back seam as far as the dotted line. Sew the back to the base, matching up the centres with the ends of the back seam and leaving a gap to turn through. Turn out, stuff and close the gap (see page 65).
2. Pin one end of the French knitting in **B** to the centre of the base (belly) and cover the whole base, winding it in a spiral and stitching as you go. Cover the back in the same way using the French knitting in **A**.
3. Sew the two heads right sides together. Turn out and fill. Close up the opening. Starting at the centre, cover the top of the head using French knitting in **B**.
4. Sew the legs together in pairs, right sides facing, leaving the straight edge open. Turn out and lightly stuff. Sew two legs to each side of the body.
5. Embroider a little pink French knot to mark each eye.

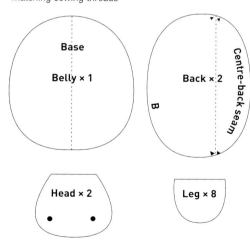

Base

Belly × 1

Back × 2

Centre-back seam

B

Head × 2

Leg × 8

5cm (2in)

PLAYFUL
PUPPETS

FRIENDLY
CREATURES

WACKY
CREATURES

CROCHETED
ANIMAL
CHARMS

7 MONKEY

SIZE: about 35cm (13¾in) high

MATERIALS

DK (sport) weight yarn (25% wool/25% acrylic/50% polyamide): 1 ball each of light brown (**A**) and mid brown (**B**)
DK (sport) weight yarn (50% wool/50% acrylic): 1 ball each of pink (**C**), red (**D**), white (**E**) and orange (**F**)
Dark orange and black embroidery thread/yarn
Synthetic filling
2.5cm (US size 1) knitting needles or size needed to obtain tension (gauge)

STITCHES

Stocking stitch (st st): knit right-side rows; purl wrong-side rows.
Chevrons:
Row 1: 1 edge st, *k3 into the next st (k into the front, k into the back, k into the front of the same stitch), k4, sl1, k2tog, psso, k4* 1 edge st.
Row 2: Purl.
Row 3: Repeat row 1.
Row 4: Knit.
Repeat these four rows.

TENSION (GAUGE)

30 sts and 40 rows = 10cm (4in).

INSTRUCTIONS

Referring to the grid patterns, knit the following in st st:
In **A**: one face, one chin, two ears and two soles.
In **B**: two heads, two ears, one base of head, two legs and two arms.

Dress × 2

Cast on 33 sts in **F**. Knit in chevrons: 6 rows **F**, 2 rows **E**, 6 rows **D**. Cont. in plain st st using **C**.
Dec 1 st at each end of rows 35, 43, 47, 51, 55, 57, 59 and 61, at the same time changing to **B** on row 47. Cast off the 17 sts remaining on row 62.

ASSEMBLY

Head: Join each **A** ear to a **B** ear, stitching around the curved edges and leaving the bottom, straight edge open. Pin an ear to each side edge of one head piece. Sew the two heads together, catching in the ears in the sewing and leaving the bottom open. Fill and sew the base in place to close the opening to the head.
Face: Close up the dart in the chin. Stitch the face to the chin along the seam at lip level. Pin then sew the whole face on to the front of the head, slipping some filling underneath and lining up the bottom of the chin with the bottom of the head. Mark the lips in dark orange backstitch. Embroider the eyes in black and white and the nostrils in red.

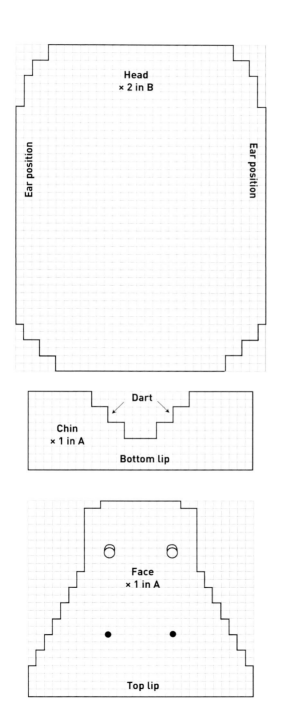

Head
× 2 in B

Ear position

Ear position

Chin
× 1 in A

Dart

Bottom lip

Face
× 1 in A

Top lip

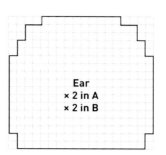

Ear
× 2 in A
× 2 in B

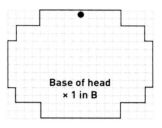

Base of head
× 1 in B

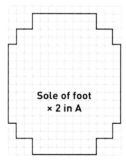

Sole of foot
× 2 in A

A = light brown
B = mid brown

MONKEY (continued)

Arms: Fold each arm in half lengthways and join the long edges, starting at the narrow end, and working on round the wide section of the hand. Stuff the hands. Close each hand, placing the vertical seam in the centre of the back.

Legs: Fold each leg in half lengthways and join the long edges, starting at the narrow end and working down and round the foot. Attach the sole of each foot. Stuff the feet. Close up the top of the legs in a flat line with the seam centred on top.

Dress: Using chain stitch in **C**, embroider two dress straps on each dress piece. Join the dress pieces at the side seams, catching the top of the arms into the seam two rows from the neck.

Final assembly: Sew the top of the dress to the base of the head. Sew the tops of the legs beneath the front edge of the dress, against the side seams.

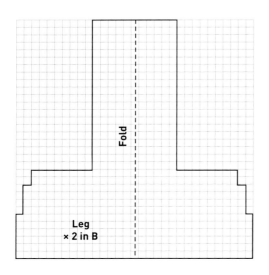

Fold

Leg
× 2 in B

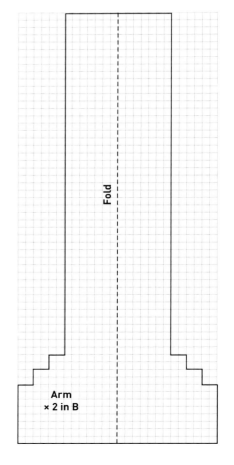

Fold

Arm
× 2 in B

8 LION

SIZE: about 40cm (15¾in) high

MATERIALS

DK (sport) weight yarn (50% wool/50% acrylic): 1 ball each
of light brown (**A**), white (**B**), light blue (**C**) and orange (**D**)
Two 16 × 20cm (6¼ × 8in) rectangles of bright yellow
polar fleece
Dark brown embroidery thread/yarn
Synthetic filling
2.5cm (US size 1) knitting needles or size needed to
obtain tension (gauge)

STITCHES

Garter stitch: knit every row.
Stocking stitch (st st): knit right-side rows; purl wrong-
side rows.

TENSION (GAUGE)

30 sts and 40 rows = 10cm (4in).

INSTRUCTIONS

Referring to the grid patterns, knit the following in st st:
In **A**: one of each side-head piece, one forehead/top of
head, one base of head, four arms, two leg fronts, two leg
backs and two soles of feet.
In **A**, **B** and **C**: two bodies/costumes, using garter stitch for the
first band in **B** and stocking stitch for the remaining pattern.

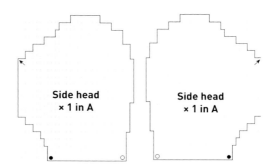

Side head
× 1 in A

Side head
× 1 in A

Tail: Cast on 19 sts in **A**. Knit 68 rows in st st and cast off.
Ears (× 2): Cast on 13 sts in **A**. Knit 20 rows in st st and
cast off.

ASSEMBLY

Head: Join the two side-head pieces, from the arrow
(nose) to the black dot (neck). Sew the forehead/top of
head between the two parts, lining up the marks. Stuff
and attach the base to close up the head opening.
Ears: Fold each ear in half lengthways and join the side
edges, rounding the corners slightly at each end of the
fold. Lightly fill. Sew an ear on to each side of the head,
5cm (2in) from the tip of the nose.

PLAYFUL
PUPPETS

FRIENDLY
CREATURES

WACKY
CREATURES

CROCHETED
ANIMAL
CHARMS

LION (continued)

Mane: Enlarge the pattern for the mane (see page 65). Cut it out twice from polar fleece. Place the two pieces wrong sides together and sew them up as indicated in the pattern, using a large running stitch and **D**. Slip some filling between the two thicknesses, then sew the mane to the top of the head, behind the ears, slightly pulling apart the edges to give some volume.

Facial features: Embroider the eyes in satin stitch using brown embroidery thread, the nose in satin stitch using **D** and the whiskers in backstitch using **D**.

Tail: Fold the tail in half lengthways and join the side seam. Close up one end of the tail, placing the seam you have just made at the side.

Arms: Put the arms together in pairs with right sides facing and stitch up the long side seams. Close up the wide end and turn right sides out. Close up the top (narrow) end.

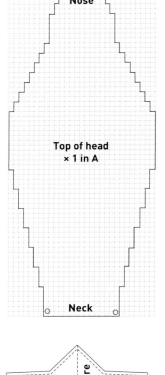

Nose

Top of head
× 1 in A

Neck

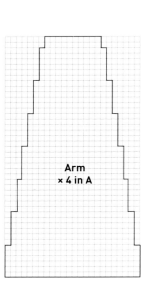

Arm
× 4 in A

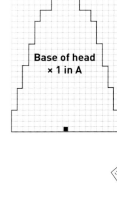

Base of head
× 1 in A

Running stitch
in D

Centre

5cm (2in)

Mane × 2

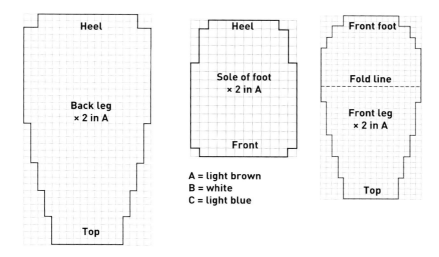

Heel

Back leg
× 2 in A

Top

Heel

Sole of foot
× 2 in A

Front

A = light brown
B = white
C = light blue

Front foot

Fold line

Front leg
× 2 in A

Top

Legs: With right sides facing sew the front to the back of each leg along the side seams. Attach the soles. Turn right sides out, fill and close up the top, placing the seams to the sides. To give more movement to the paw, sew some stitches through all the layers along the fold line.

Body/costume: Embroider the lines on the costume in chain stitch using **C**. Join the two body pieces along the side seams, catching the tops of the arms into the seam two rows from the neck.

Final assembly: Sew the top of the body/costume on to the bottom of the head. Sew the tail to the centre of stripe A on the back of the costume. Sew the tops of the legs beneath the front edge of the costume, against the side seams.

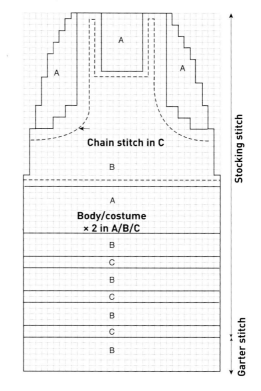

A

A   A

Chain stitch in C

B

A
Body/costume
× 2 in A/B/C

B

C

B

C

B

C

B

Stocking stitch

Garter stitch

PLAYFUL PUPPETS

FRIENDLY CREATURES

WACKY CREATURES

CROCHETED ANIMAL CHARMS

9 GIRAFFE

SIZE: about 45cm (17¾in) high

MATERIALS

Merino DK (sport) weight wool yarn: 1 ball of deep orange (**A**)
4-ply (fingering) weight yarn (30% lambswool/70% acrylic): 1 ball each of mid green (**B**) and light brown (**C**)
Dark brown embroidery thread/yarn
Synthetic filling
3mm (US size 3) knitting needles or size needed to obtain tension (gauge)
2.5mm (US size 1/C) crochet hook

STITCHES

Garter stitch: knit every row.
Stocking stitch (st st): knit right-side rows; purl wrong-side rows.
Crochet: foundation chain (ch), slip stitch (sl st) and US single crochet/UK double crochet (see page 64).

TENSION (GAUGE)

30 sts and 24 rows = 10cm (4in).

INSTRUCTIONS

Referring to the grid patterns, knit the following in st st:
In **A**: one head and one of each neck piece.
In **C**: two muzzles, two ears.
In **A** and **B**: two bodies/costumes.

Arms and legs (× 4)**:** Cast on 13 sts in **A**. Knit 38 rows in st st and cast off.
Hooves (× 4)**:** Cast on 43 sts in **C**. Knit 24 rows in st st and cast off.
Mane: Cast on 90 sts in **C**. Knit 4 rows in garter stitch, then 6 rows in st st.
Row 11: K2tog; repeat to end of row [45 sts]. Cast off.

Spots: Using **C**, 4ch and join with sl st into a ring.

Round 1: 1ch, 8sc (*UK dc*) into the ring, join with sl st into the ch at start of round [8 sts].

Round 2: 1ch then 2sc (*UK dc*) into each sc (*UK dc*) [16 sts].

Round 3: 1ch, *1sc (*UK dc*) into the next sc (*UK dc*), 2sc (*UK dc*) into the following sc (*UK dc*)*; repeat from * to * all around, sl st into the ch at start of round [24 sts]. Fasten off.

Crochet 6 spots with 3 rounds and 6 spots with 2 round.

Horns (× 2): Using **C**, 10ch. sl st into each of the first 3 ch, 1sc (*UK dc*) into each of the following 7 ch. Fasten off.

ASSEMBLY

Ears: Fold each ear along the fold line and join the first and last rows; join the rounded edge. Pin the open straight edge of each ear to the centre of the cast-off row of each part of the neck.

Head: Join the top of each neck to one side of the head, matching the marks and catching the ear into each seam. Pin the cast-off row of the mane to one neck, right sides together, and on to the last seven stitches of the top of the head (on one side of the dart), gathering slightly if necessary. Place the other neck on top, right sides together, then sew along the length and close up the top dart. Close the front edge of the neck from the base to the triangle.

Muzzle: Close the darts for the two pieces of the muzzle. Sew the two parts together, right sides facing, along the narrowest edge (where the dart is). Join the side edges together. Sew the muzzle to the front of the head, placing the seams level with the seams between the neck and the head, and insert the end of the muzzle into the neck as far as the triangle. Stuff the head and neck and close up the base of the neck.

Facial features: Embroider the eyes and nostrils in brown embroidery thread/yarn using satin stitch. Mark the mouth with backstitch using the same colour.

Legs and arms: Fold each piece lengthways and join the long edges. Close up the ends. Join the side edges of each hoof. Sew a gathering yarn on to the cast-off row and the cast-on row of each hoof. Pull up one of the two yarns and stuff the hoof. Pull up the other yarn and secure the end. Sew one hoof to the end of each arm or leg.

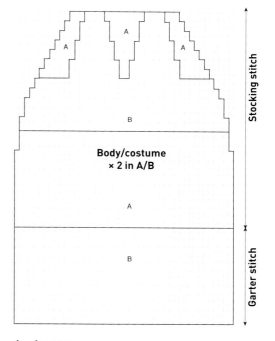

A = deep orange
B = mid green
C = light brown

Body/costume: Join the sides of the body/costume pieces, catching the tops of the arms into each seam. Sew the top of the body/costume on to the base of the neck. Sew the tops of the legs beneath the front edge of the body/costume, 2cm (¾in) from each side seams.

Spots: Distribute the spots over the head, neck and tummy and sew on firmly.

PLAYFUL PUPPETS

FRIENDLY CREATURES

WACKY CREATURES

CROCHETED ANIMAL CHARMS

GIRAFFE (continued)

A = deep orange
B = mid green
C = light brown

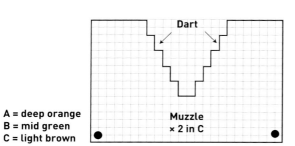
Dart

Muzzle
× 2 in C

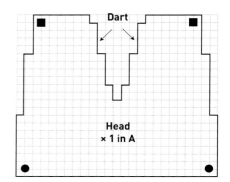
Dart

Head
× 1 in A

Ear
× 2 in C

Fold line

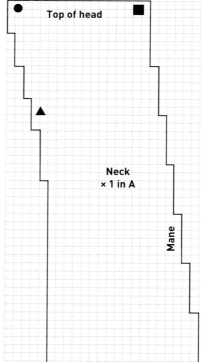
Top of head

Neck
× 1 in A

Mane

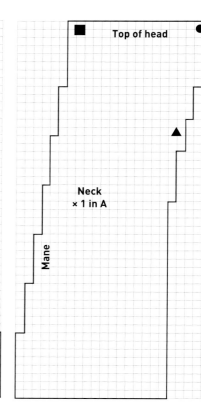
Top of head

Neck
× 1 in A

Mane

10 HIPPOPOTAMUS

SIZE: about 30cm (12in) high

MATERIALS

4-ply (fingering) weight yarn (30% lambswool/70% acrylic): 1 ball each of light green (**A**) and pale turquoise (**B**)
DK (sport) weight yarn (50% wool/50% acrylic): 1 ball each of orange (**C**) and deep pink (**D**)
Synthetic filling
Navy-blue embroidery thread/yarn
2.5cm (US size 1) knitting needles or size needed to obtain tension (gauge)

STITCHES

Garter stitch: knit every row.
Stocking stitch (st st): knit right-side rows; purl wrong-side rows.

Note when decreasing, k2tog one stitch away from each edge.

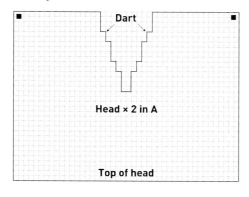

Dart

Head × 2 in A

Top of head

TENSION (GAUGE)

30 sts and 40 rows = 10cm (4in).

INSTRUCTIONS

Referring to the grid patterns, knit the following in st st unless otherwise stated:
In **A**: two heads, two paws for the arms and two paws for the legs.
In **B**: one bottom muzzle (chin), one top muzzle, two arms, two legs and two bodies, noting that the bottom band of the body is worked in garter stitch.
Ears (× 2)**:** Cast on 9 sts in **B**. Knit 12 rows in st st. Now work 12 rows of st st in **A** and cast off.
Pocket: Cast on 26 sts in **D**. Knit 16 rows in st st then 5 rows in garter st; cast off.

ASSEMBLY

Head: Close up the dart on each head piece then join the pieces together along the top seam (cast-on edge). Join the sides.
Muzzle: Close up the dart on the top and bottom muzzle pieces. Join the two pieces (the bottom piece is longer). Sew the muzzle to the head, sewing the excess from the bottom piece to the base of the back of the head, leaving an opening. Stuff the head and close the opening.
Ears: Fold the ears in half and join the sides. Slip in a little filling. Sew the base of each ear along the joining seam for the two parts of the head, leaving it slightly open to give volume to the ear. Use backstitch and arrange the ears with colour **B** to the front.

PLAYFUL PUPPETS

FRIENDLY CREATURES

WACKY CREATURES

CROCHETED ANIMAL CHARMS

HIPPOPOTAMUS (continued)

Facial features: Using navy thread, embroider the nostrils in satin stitch and the mouth in backstitch with satin stitch at the ends; work a French knot for each eye.

Arms and legs: Fold each piece lengthways and join the edges. Insert the paw into the widest end and stuff each limb. Close the end by stitching flat, placing the vertical seam of the legs in the centre of the front, with the seam of the arms towards the back.

Body: Attach the pocket to the centre front. Join the sides, catching the tops of the arms into the tops of the seams. Close up the shoulders for eight stitches. Sew the twelve centre stitches of the back and the front, slightly spaced apart, under the head. Sew the tops of the legs beneath the front edge of the body, level with the side seams.

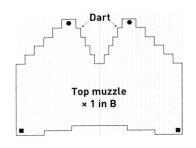

Dart

Top muzzle
× 1 in B

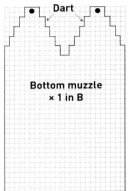

Dart

Bottom muzzle
× 1 in B

A = light green
B = pale turquoise
C = orange
D = deep pink

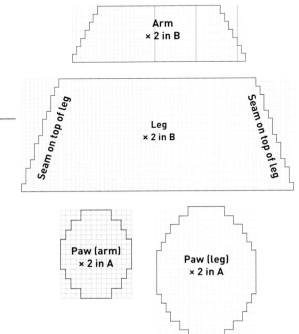

Arm
× 2 in B

Seam on top of leg

Leg
× 2 in B

Seam on top of leg

Paw (arm)
× 2 in A

Paw (leg)
× 2 in A

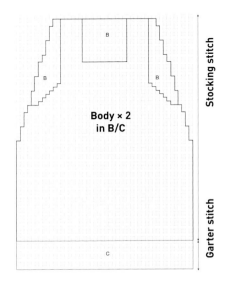

B

B   B

Body × 2
in B/C

C

Stocking stitch

Garter stitch

FRIENDLY CREATURES

WACKY CREATURES

CROCHETED ANIMAL CHARMS

11 POLAR BEAR

SIZE: about 25cm (10in) high

MATERIALS

Soft textured DK (sport) weight yarn (100% polyester): 1 ball of cream (**A**)
DK (sport) weight yarn (25% wool/25% acrylic/ 50% polyamide): 1 ball of black (**B**)
Synthetic filling
2.5cm (US size 1) and 3mm (US size 3) knitting needles or size needed to obtain tension (gauge)

STITCHES

Stocking stitch (st st): knit right-side rows; purl wrong-side rows.

TENSION (GAUGE)

26 sts and 34 rows using 3mm (US size 3) needles = 10cm (4in) and 34 rows.

INSTRUCTIONS

Referring to the grid patterns, knit the following in st st:
In **A**: one top of head, one of each side head, one muzzle, four ears, two of each arm piece, two of each leg piece, one of each body piece, one tummy and two tails, all using 3mm (US size 3) knitting needles.
In **B**: four paws using 2.5mm (US size 1) knitting needles.

ASSEMBLY

Head: Sew the top of the head between the sides of the head, matching the marks. Close up the neck but leave the opening for the muzzle. Stuff the head. Sew the ears together in pairs then sew them to each side of the head.
Muzzle: Fold the muzzle and join the slanted edge. Join up the side edges then fill with stuffing. Flatten the muzzle on to the head and sew in place.

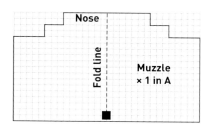

Nose
Fold line
Muzzle
× 1 in A

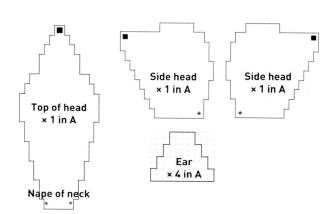

Top of head
× 1 in A

Nape of neck

Side head
× 1 in A

Side head
× 1 in A

Ear
× 4 in A

POLAR BEAR (continued)

Body: Attach the tummy between the two parts of the body, matching the marks and then sew the two parts of the body together along the centre-back seam. Check that there are no holes in the bottom; fill. Sew the head on to the body.

Tail: Sew the two parts of the tail together leaving the base (wide end) open. Slip a little filling inside and stitch the opening closed. Attach the tail to the body.

Arms: Sew the arms together in pairs, leaving the top and bottom open. Attach a paw to the wide end. Stuff each arm.

Back legs: Sew the legs together as for the arms. Sew the legs horizontally to the sides of the back, 4cm (1½in) from the centre-back seam, so that they support the bear. Sew the arms to the front, 3cm (1¼in) apart, so that they touch the ground between the legs.

Facial features: Using B, embroider the eyes and then the nose in satin stitch. Mark in the mouth using backstitch.

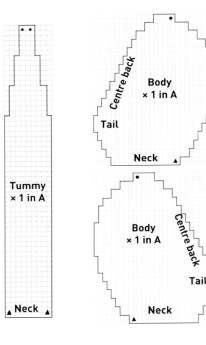

Tummy × 1 in A
Neck

Body × 1 in A
Centre back
Tail
Neck

Body × 1 in A
Centre back
Tail
Neck

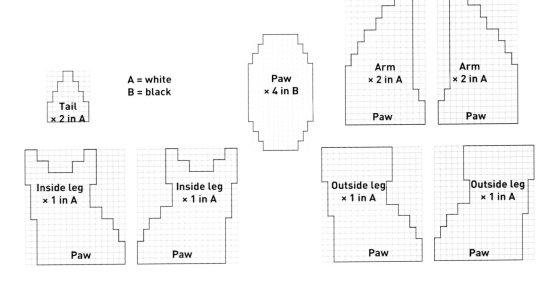

A = white
B = black

Tail × 2 in A

Paw × 4 in B

Arm × 2 in A
Paw

Arm × 2 in A
Paw

Inside leg × 1 in A
Paw

Inside leg × 1 in A
Paw

Outside leg × 1 in A
Paw

Outside leg × 1 in A
Paw

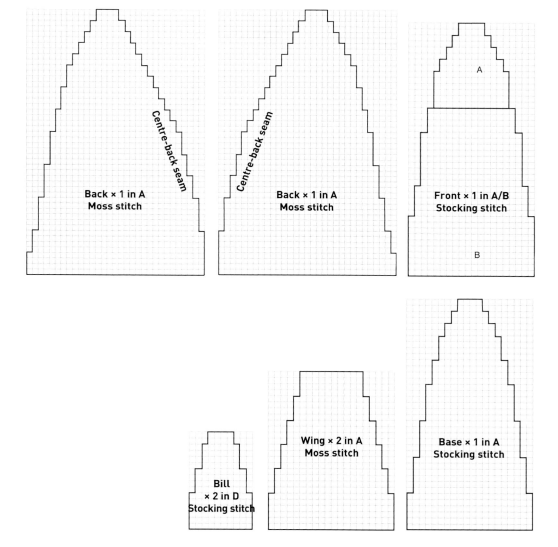

Back × 1 in A
Moss stitch

Centre-back seam

Back × 1 in A
Moss stitch

Centre-back seam

Front × 1 in A/B
Stocking stitch

A

B

Bill
× 2 in D
Stocking stitch

Wing × 2 in A
Moss stitch

Base × 1 in A
Stocking stitch

FRIENDLY CREATURES

WACKY CREATURES

CROCHETED ANIMAL CHARMS

16 ZEBRA

SIZE: about 22cm (8¾in) high

MATERIALS

DK (sport) weight yarn (50% wool/50% acrylic): 1 ball each of black (**A**) and white (**B**)
Synthetic filling
2.5mm (US size 1) knitting needles or size needed to obtain tension (gauge)

STITCHES

Stocking stitch (st st): knit right-side rows; purl wrong-side rows.
Striped stocking stitch: *2 rows **B**, 2 rows **A***; repeat from * to * as instructed.
Moss stitch (see page 64).

TENSION (GAUGE)

30 sts and 40 rows = 10cm (4in).

INSTRUCTIONS

The zebra is made from just rectangles and therefore does not require any grids.

Body (× 2): Cast on 28 sts in **B**. Knit 60 rows in striped st st. Cast off.
Head (× 2): Cast on 21 sts in **B**. Knit 32 rows in striped st st. Cast off.
Legs (× 4): Cast on 12 sts in **B**. Knit 24 rows in st st. Cast off.
Muzzle (× 1): Cast on 36 sts in **B**. Knit 36 rows in st st. Cast off.
Hooves (× 4): Cast on 38 sts in **A**. Knit 22 rows in st st. Cast off.
Ears (× 2): Cast on 11 sts in **A**. Knit 26 rows in st st. Cast off.
Tail (× 1): Cast on 20 sts in **A**. Knit 8 rows in st st. Cast off.
Mane (× 1): Cast on 80 sts in **A**. Knit 4 rows in moss stitch then cont. in st st.
On row 7 *k2tog; repeat from * to the end of the row. Knit another 4 rows using the remaining 40 sts; cast off.

ASSEMBLY

Head: Place the head pieces together with right sides facing and join one side edge. Sew the muzzle to one end of the head, aligning the centre of the cast-on row of the muzzle to the joining seam on the head (the muzzle is narrower than the head). Fold the head, right sides together, along the seam. Close up the end of the muzzle, rounding off the corners, then close up the underneath of the muzzle and the underneath of the head for five stripes, at a slight angle to meet up with the width of the head; turn the head right sides out. Slip the cast-on row of the mane between the cast-on rows of the back of the head, gathering, then sew firmly.

Body: Place the two pieces right sides together. Sew the side seams, leaving an opening in the top seam, towards the front, that has the same number of stripes as the base of the head. Close up the front end, slightly rounding the bottom of the seam. Close up the rear end in the same way, leaving an opening in the top.

Attaching the head: Sew the base of the head to the top of the body matching up the stripes. Fill the body and the head. Close up the opening.

Ears: Fold each ear right sides together along row 13. Close up the sides, rounding off the corners at the top (folded edge); turn out. Sew an ear on to each side of the head, positioned towards the back, 3cm (1¼in) up and 2cm (¾in) from the rear seam.

Tail: Fold the tail wrong sides together to sew the cast-on row to the cast-off row. Close up the ends. Sew the tail in position on the body.

Legs and hooves: Fold each leg wrong sides together between stitches 6 and 7. Close up the length; turn out. Join each hoof into a ring, sewing the side edges together. Thread a gathering thread into the cast-on row and the cast-off row. Gather one of the edges and finish off firmly; stuff each hoof. Gather and close up the other edge. Sew a hoof on to one end of each leg. Sew the legs on to each side of the body.

Facial features: Embroider using **A**: the eyes and the nostrils in long stitch and the mouth using backstitch.

17 FAT CAT

SIZE: about 30cm (12in) high

MATERIALS

DK (sport) weight yarn (25% wool/25% acrylic/50% polyamide): 1 ball each of cream (**A**) and dark brown (**B**) soft textured chunky 100% polyester yarn: 1 ball of cream (**C**)
Synthetic filling
3mm (US size 3) and 4.5mm (US size 7) knitting needles or size needed to obtain tension (gauge)
5mm (US size H) crochet hook

STITCHES

Stocking stitch (st st): knit right-side rows; purl wrong-side rows.
Crochet: foundation chain (ch) and slip stitch (sl st); see page 64.

TENSION (GAUGE)

15 sts and 27 rows of stocking stitch using 4.5mm (US size 7) needles = 10cm (4in).

INSTRUCTIONS

Referring to the grid patterns, knit the following in st st:
In **B** with 3mm (US size 3) knitting needles: two heads.
In **C** with 4.5mm (US size 7) knitting needles: two ears.
Body: Cast on 44 sts in **C** using 4.5mm (US size 7) knitting needles. Knit 13cm (5in) in st st and cast off.
Legs and arms (× 4): Cast on 24 sts in **B** using 3mm (US size 3) knitting needles. Knit 4.5cm (1¾in) in st st and cast off.

Tail: Crochet a 20cm (8in) chain using **C**. Turn and work back to the start with sl st into each stitch; finish off.

ASSEMBLY

Body: Join the side edges of the body. Thread a gathering thread into the cast-on row. Pull up and finish off firmly. Thread a gathering thread into the cast-off row; stuff the body but do not close the opening yet.
Head: Sew the two parts of the head together, leaving the base (cast-on edge) open; stuff the head. Gather the top of the body to reduce it to the same size as the base of the head. Attach the head to the body. Sew an ear to each side of the head.
Facial features: Embroider the nose in satin stitch using A. Add the whiskers and eyes using long stitches in the same yarn.
Limbs: Join the side edges of each arm and of each leg. Thread a gathering thread into the cast-on row of each limb and pull up. Finish off firmly. Stuff the limbs and sew them to each side of the body. Attach the tail to the rear.

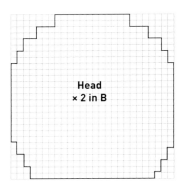

Head
× 2 in B

Ear
× 2 in C

18 BLACK DOG

SIZE: about 18cm (7in) high

MATERIALS

DK (sport) weight yarn (100% cotton): 2 balls of black (**A**) and 1 ball of white (**B**)
Synthetic filling
2.5mm (US size 1) knitting needles or size needed to obtain tension (gauge)
2.5mm (US size 1/C) crochet hook

STITCHES

Stocking stitch (st st): knit right-side rows; purl wrong-side rows.
Crochet: foundation chain (ch), slip stitch (sl st) and US single crochet/UK double crochet (see page 64).

TENSION (GAUGE)

25 sts and 38 rows of stocking stitch = 10cm (4in).

INSTRUCTIONS

Referring to the grid patterns on page 97, knit the following in st st:
In **A**: five heads, four arms, one of each back piece, one front and one base.
In **B**: two tails.
Ears: Cast on 8 sts in B. Knit 28 rows in plain st st and cast off.
Eye patch: Using **B**, make a loop of yarn around your finger. Work 4sc (*UK dc*) into the loop. Pull on the yarn to close the loop. Then work sc (*UK dc*) in rounds without turning:

Round 1: 2sc (*UK dc*) into each stitch all around [8 sts].
Round 2: *sc (*UK dc*) into the next sc (*UK dc*), 2sc (*UK dc*) into the following sc (*UK dc*)*; repeat from * to * all around [12 sts].
Round 3: *sc (*UK dc*) into the next sc (*UK dc*), 2sc (*UK dc*) into the following sc (*UK dc*)*; repeat from * to * all around [18 sts]. Fasten off and darn in the end.

ASSEMBLY

Head: Sew together the five parts of the head along the long curved edges, ensuring that the top is properly closed. One of the five segments forms the rear of the head, two form the front (with a centre seam), and the remaining two form the sides. Leave the neck open and fill.
Ears: Fold each ear in half and stitch the side seams. Stitch the base of each ear on to a side head segment, 5cm (2in) from the top, using backstitch.
Facial features: Using **B** doubled, embroider the nose and one eye in satin stitch. Use the same yarn, this time just one strand, to embroider the mouth in backstitch. Sew on the crocheted patch firmly using **B**; mark the eye on top using satin stitch in **A**.
Body: Join the two parts of the back along the centre-back seam. Sew the front between the two back pieces. Add the base. Fill via the neck.
Arms: Sew the arms together in pairs leaving the base open. Lightly fill. Sew an arm to each side of the body in line with the neck.
Finishing: Sew together the two parts of the tail and sew across the seam at the base of the back.
Sew the head to the body.

19 WHITE DOG

SIZE: about 18cm (7in) high

MATERIALS

DK (sport) weight yarn (100% cotton): 1 ball of black (**A**), 2 balls of white (**B**)
Synthetic filling
2.5mm (US size 1) knitting needles or size needed to obtain tension (gauge)
2.5mm (US size 1/C) crochet hook

STITCHES

Stocking stitch (st st): knit right-side rows; purl wrong-side rows.
Crochet: foundation chain (ch), slip stitch (sl st) and US single crochet/UK double crochet (see page 64).

TENSION (GAUGE)

25 sts and 38 rows of stocking stitch = 10cm (4in).

INSTRUCTIONS

Referring to the grid patterns, knit the following in st st:
In **B**: five heads, four arms, one of each back piece, one front and one base.
In **A**: two tails.

Ears
Cast on 8 sts in **A**. Knit 28 rows in st st and cast off.

Eye patch
Using **A**, make a loop of yarn around your finger. Work 4sc (*UK dc*) into the loop. Pull on the yarn to close the loop. Then work sc (*UK dc*) in rounds without turning:

Round 1: 2sc (*UK dc*) into each stitch around [8 sts].
Round 2: *sc (*UK dc*) into the next sc (*UK dc*), 2sc (*UK dc*) into the following sc* (*UK dc*); repeat from * to * all around [12 sts].
Round 3: *sc (*UK dc*) into the next sc (*UK dc*), 2sc (*UK dc*) into the following sc* (*UK dc*); repeat from * to * all around [18 sts]. Fasten off and darn in the end.

ASSEMBLY

Head: Sew together the five parts of the head along the long curved edges, ensuring that the top is properly closed. One of the five segments forms the rear of the head, two the front (with a centre seam), and the remaining two form the sides. Leave the neck open and fill.
Ears: Fold each ear in half and stitch the side seams. Stitch the base of each ear on to a side head segment, 5cm (2in) from the top, using backstitch.
Facial features: Using **A** doubled, embroider the nose and one eye in satin stitch. Use the same yarn, this time just one strand, to embroider the mouth in backstitch. Sew on the crocheted patch firmly using **A**; mark the eye on top using satin stitch in **B**.
Body: Join the two parts of the back along the centre-back seam. Sew the front between the two back pieces. Add the base. Fill via the neck.
Arms: Sew the arms together in pairs, leaving the base open. Lightly fill and then close the gap. Sew an arm to each side of the body in line with the neck.
Finishing: Sew the two parts of the tail together and attach it across the seam at the base of the back. Sew the head to the body.

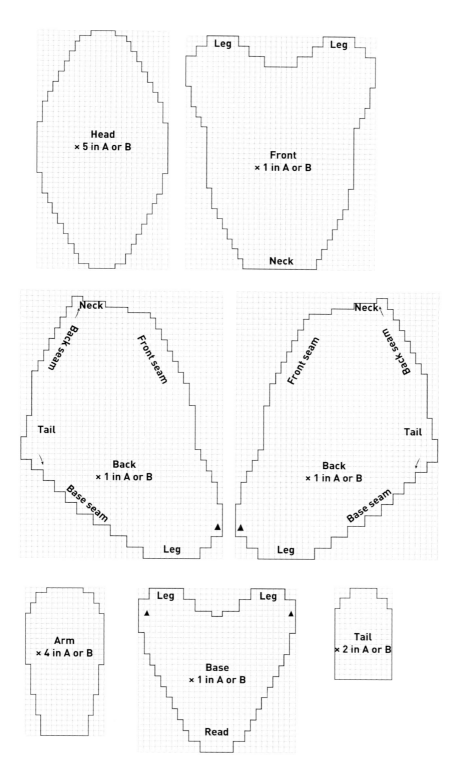

Head
× 5 in A or B

Leg   Leg

Front
× 1 in A or B

Neck

Neck

Back seam   Front seam

Tail

Back
× 1 in A or B

Base seam

▲

Leg

Neck

Front seam   Back seam

Tail

Back
× 1 in A or B

▲

Base seam

Leg

Arm
× 4 in A or B

Leg   Leg

▲   ▲

Base
× 1 in A or B

Read

Tail
× 2 in A or B

FRIENDLY
CREATURES

WACKY
CREATURES

CROCHETED
ANIMAL
CHARMS

20 CUDDLY CAT

SIZE: about 45cm (17¾in) long

MATERIALS

Soft, elastic DK (sport) weight baby yarn: 1 ball each of white (**A**) and mid grey (**B**)
DK (sport) weight yarn (25% wool/25% acrylic/50% polyamide): 1 ball of mid grey (**C**)
Synthetic filling
3mm (US size 3) and 5mm (US size 8) knitting needles or sizes needed to obtain tension (gauge)
4mm (US size G) crochet hook

STITCHES

Stocking stitch (st st): knit right-side rows; purl wrong-side rows.
Crochet: foundation chain (ch) and slip stitch (sl st).

TENSION (GAUGE)

25 sts and 34 rows of stocking stitch in DK (sport) weight yarn using 3mm (US size 2) knitting needles = 10cm (4in).
24 sts and 38 rows of stocking stitch in baby yarn using 5mm (US size 8) needles = 10cm (4in) square.

INSTRUCTIONS

Referring to the grid patterns, knit the following in st st using 5mm (US size 8) needles:
In **A** and **B**: two front/back pieces; in **B**: two ears.
Arms (× 2): Cast on 16 sts in **A**, using 5mm (US size 8) knitting needles, and knit in st st for 3cm (1¼in). Change to 3mm (US size 3) needles and knit in st st using **C** for

12cm (4¾in); cast off.
Legs (× 2): Cast on 16 sts in **A**, using 5mm (US size 8) knitting needles, and knit in st st for 4cm (1½in). Change to 3mm (US size 3) needles and knit in st st using **C** for 16cm (6¼in); cast off.
Tail: Using **B**, 52ch. Turn and work back to the start with sl st into each ch; finish off.

ASSEMBLY

Limbs: Fold each arm and each leg in half lengthways and join the side seam. Gather the cast-on edge (in **A**); fill. Close the top of each limb flat.
Body: Place front and back right sides together. Slip arms and legs in place between the two thicknesses so that they will be on the outside when the body is turned out. Sew all round, leaving an opening under one arm to turn through; turn out. Stuff the cat and close up. Sew on the ears.
Face: Embroider nose and eyes in satin stitch using **C**. Add whiskers with straight stitch using same yarn.
Finishing: Gather the last row of **A** where it joins **C** on each limb using a gathering thread in **A** to mark the feet and hands. Sew on the tail.

Ears
× 2 in B

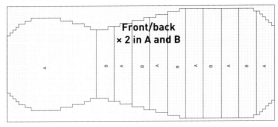

Front/back
× 2 in A and B

WACKY CREATURES

CROCHETED ANIMAL CHARMS

21 FANFAN THE ELEPHANT

SIZE: about 30cm (12in) high

MATERIALS

DK (sport) weight yarn (50% wool/50% acrylic): 1 ball of white (**A**) and 2 balls pale pink (**B**)
4-ply (fingering) weight yarn (30% lambswool/70% acrylic): 1 ball of deep pink (**C**) and 2 balls deep peach (**D**)
3mm (US size 3) and 4mm (US size 6) knitting needles or size needed to obtain tension (gauge)

STITCHES USED

Garter stitch: knit every row.
Stocking stitch (st st): knit right-side rows; purl wrong-side rows.
Note: Decreasing the legs and trunk is done on the right side of the work two stitches away from the edge: at the start of the row, k2 then sl1, k1 psso; at the end of the row when there are four stitches left on the left needle, k2tog and k2.
psso: pass the slipped stitch over the knitted stitch.

TENSION (GAUGE)

26 sts and 35 rows of stocking stitch using 3mm (US size 3) knitting needles = 10cm (4in).

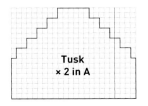
Tusk
× 2 in A

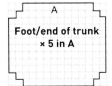
A
Foot/end of trunk
× 5 in A

INSTRUCTIONS

Referring to the grid patterns, knit the following in st st unless otherwise stated:
In **A** with 3mm (US size 3) knitting needles: two tusks, four feet and one trunk end.
In **B** with 3mm (US size 3) knitting needles: one trunk/forehead, one of each side-head piece and one leg.
In **C** with 3mm (US size 3) knitting needles: two legs.
In **D** with 3mm (US size 3) knitting needles: one leg.
In **D** with 4mm (US size 6) knitting needles: two ears in garter stitch using double yarn.

Body

Cast on 45 sts in **B**. Using the yarn doubled and 4mm (US size 6) knitting needles, knit 6 rows in st st, then 14 rows in garter stitch. Change to **D** and knit *4 rows st st, 14 rows garter stitch*. Repeat from * to * once using **C**, once using **B** and once more using **D**. Finally knit 6 rows of st st and cast off.
Tail: Cast on 36 sts. Using **D** (not doubled) and 3mm (US size 3) knitting needles, knit 8 rows in garter stitch and cast off.

ASSEMBLY

Legs: Fold each leg in half lengthways and join the sides. Insert the foot into the end. Slip some filling into the bottom of the legs. Embroider the nails in satin stitch using **A**. Gather up the top to close up.

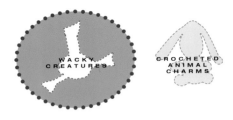

ELEPHANT (continued)

Head: Attach a side-head piece to each side of the forehead (top of trunk piece), matching the marks. Close up the trunk by sewing the edges together. Insert the trunk end. Close up the head beneath the chin (from the black triangle to the black square). Sew the cast-off row of the ears on to each side of the head.

Tusks: Fold each tusk in half and stitch the shaped edges together, leaving the cast-on row open. Lightly fill. Sew one tusk to each side of the head.

Eyes: Embroider two little eyes to the face just above the tusks in satin stitch using **D**.

Body: Close the body up into a ring by sewing the edges together. Make the folds of flesh by folding the garter-stitch parts wrong sides together and joining the first and last rows by stitching on the reverse.

Attaching the legs: Run a gathering thread through the cast-on row of the body. Slip the tops of the legs into the end of the body and pull the gathering thread tight. Finish off firmly. Hold the legs in place with stitches inside the body.

Attaching the head: Fill the body. Slip the end of the head into the top of the body, then sew the body firmly around the base of the head.

A = white
B = pale pink
C = deep pink
D = deep peach

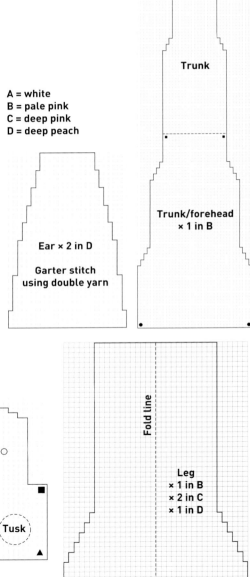

Trunk

Trunk/forehead
× 1 in B

Ear × 2 in D

Garter stitch
using double yarn

Fold line

Leg
× 1 in B
× 2 in C
× 1 in D

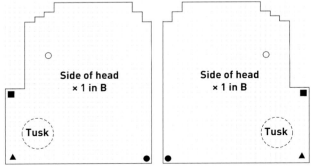

Side of head
× 1 in B

Side of head
× 1 in B

Tusk

Tusk

22 ANTOINETTE THE LITTLE HEN

SIZE: about 32cm (12½in) high

MATERIALS

DK (sport) weight yarn (100% cotton): 1 ball each of white (**A**), red (**D**), orange (**C**), pale blue (**D**) and purple (**E**)
Scraps of felt or polar fleece in white and orange
Black darning thread
Orange sewing thread
Synthetic filling
2.5mm (US size 1) knitting needles or size needed to obtain tension (gauge)

STITCHES

Stocking stitch (st st): knit right-side rows; purl wrong-side rows.
Garter stitch: knit every row.

TENSION (GAUGE)

25 sts and 38 rows of stocking stitch = 10cm (4in).

INSTRUCTIONS

Referring to the grid patterns, knit the following in st st:
In **A**: one body base.
In **B**: one comb.
In **C**: four legs.
In all colours: two striped bodies with the whole section below stripe **D** in **A**.

Ruffles
Cast on 168 sts in **D**.
Rows 1–4: work in garter stitch (knit every row).
Rows 4–12: work in st st.
Row 13: k3tog to end of row [56 sts]. Cast off.
Cast on 132 sts in **B** and knit a second ruffle in the same way [44 sts at end of row 13].
Cast on 108 sts in **E** and knit a third ruffle in the same way [36 sts at end of row 13].

ASSEMBLY

Body: Join the two parts of the body together leaving the wider (cast-on) end open. Close the ruffles into rings and, using overcast stitch in **A**, sew the cast-off row to the body at the level indicated on the body pattern by the broken lines. Insert the base leaving the front end open. Stuff with filling but do not close the gap yet.
Legs: Sew the legs together in pairs, leaving the top and bottom open. Close up the bottom (cast-on edge) flat, wrong sides together using backstitch on the right side. Fill the feet, leaving the legs empty. Pin the tops of the legs beneath the front edge of the body, 3cm (1¼in) apart. Finish the seam, securing the legs.

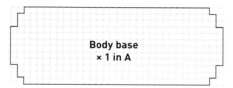

Body base
× 1 in A

HEN (continued)

Comb: Fold the comb in half lengthways as indicated on the pattern and stitch the side edges together. Press the comb flat with wrong sides together, placing the seam you've just made to one side. Close up the top flat using backstitch on the right side. Slide the comb at an angle on to the top of the head and sew in place.

Facial features: Cut two small circles of white felt or fleece and cut an orange triangle for the beak. Position them on the face. Attach each eye with a little black stitch in the centre. Sew on the beak using little stitches in orange thread or yarn, overlapping the border.

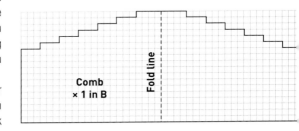

Comb
× 1 in B

Fold line

A = white
B = red
C = orange
D = pale blue
E = purple

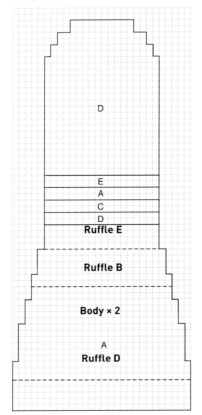

D

E
A
C
D
Ruffle E

Ruffle B

Body × 2

A
Ruffle D

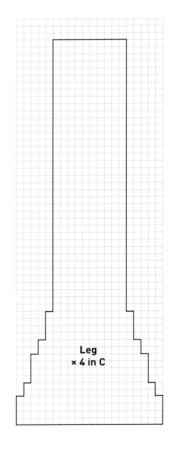

Leg
× 4 in C

23 FELIX THE MARTIAN DOG

SIZE: about 25cm (10in) high

MATERIALS

DK (sport) weight yarn (25% wool/40% acrylic/35% chlorofibre): 3 balls each of scarlet (**A**) and purple (**B**), 1 ball each of pale blue (**C**) and white (**D**)
Scraps of turquoise, bright yellow and bright red felt or polar fleece
Synthetic filling
Thread to match the felt or fleece
2.5mm (US size 1) and 5mm (US size 8) knitting needles or sizes needed to obtain tension (gauge)

STITCHES

Garter stitch: knit every row.
Stocking stitch (st st): knit right-side rows; purl wrong-side rows.

TENSION (GAUGE)

26 sts and 34 rows of stocking stitch using 2.5mm (US size 1) needles = 10cm (4in).
18 sts and 28 rows of garter stitch with double yarn and 5mm (US size 8) needles = 10cm (4in).

INSTRUCTIONS

Referring to the grid pattern, knit the whole of the back (including the head) in one piece using your yarn doubled and 5mm (US size 8) knitting needles, stitching in garter stitch. Start this piece at the top of the head with **B**, changing to **A** at the line to work the body. Knit the front in two sections, reversing the colours and casting off the stitches between the colour sections (so you can insert the scarf in the seam). In this way you will begin the front body section by casting on 32 sts in **B**.

Antennae and scarf (× 4)

Cast on 22 sts in **D** and knit in st st with a single yarn and 2.5mm (US size 1) knitting needles: *4 rows **D**, 2 rows **A**, 2 rows **B**, 2 rows **A**, 2 rows **D**, 2 rows **C**, 4 rows **B**, 2 rows **C**, 4 rows **A**, 2 rows **D**, 2 rows **B**, 2 rows **A**, 2 rows **C***. Repeat from * to *; cast off on row 93.

ASSEMBLY

Antennae and scarf: Fold each strip lengthways and join the long edges. Close one end flat, placing the seam just made in the centre underneath and stitching the seam on the right side along the edge.
Body: Pin an antenna to each side of the top of the front head piece, and a scarf section to the edge of the cast-on row. Sew together the two parts of the front, catching in the scarf sections and leaving the edge of the head showing to form a little roll. Sew together the back and the front, catching the antennae into the seam and leaving a gap. Fill and close up the gap.
Eyes: Cut two circles of turquoise felt/polar fleece, two smaller ones in bright yellow and two even smaller ones in bright red. Sew the red circles on to the yellow ones, then the yellow ones on to the turquoise ones. Sew the eyes on to the front.

MARTIAN DOG (continued)

Tip

If you are short of time, make the antennae and scarf from an existing piece of knitting or from fabric or fleece.

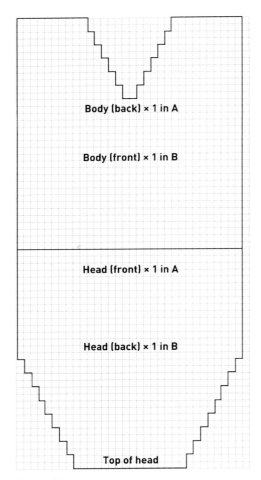

Body (back) × 1 in A

Body (front) × 1 in B

Head (front) × 1 in A

Head (back) × 1 in B

Top of head

A = scarlet
B = purple

24 BIG WOLF

SIZE: about 50cm (19¾in) high

MATERIALS

DK (sport) weight yarn (50% wool/50% acrylic): 1 ball each of dark blue (**A**), lime green (**B**), red (**C**) deep pink (**D**) and light grey (**E**)
Two circles of orange felt or polar fleece and two smaller circles of white felt or polar fleece for the eyes
Black embroidery thread/yarn
Synthetic filling
2.5mm (US size 1) knitting needles or size needed to obtain tension (gauge)

STITCHES

Stocking stitch (st st): knit right-side rows; purl wrong-side rows.

TENSION (GAUGE)

30 sts and 40 rows in st st = 10cm (4in).

INSTRUCTIONS

Referring to the grid patterns, knit the following in st st:
In **E**: two heads.
In **A**, **B**, **C** and **D**: two bodies, one tail, one right leg, one left leg, one right arm and one left arm.
Make the decreases two stitches away from the edges.
Patches: For the large patch, cast on 15 sts in **E**. Knit 16 rows in plain st st and cast off.
For the small patch, cast on 12 sts in **E**. Knit 12 rows in plain st st and cast off.

Tail × 1

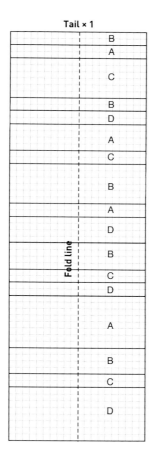

B
A
C
B
D
A
C
B
A
D
B
C
D

Fold line

A
B
C
D

ASSEMBLY

Legs, arms and tail: Fold each leg in half lengthways, with right sides facing. Stitch the side seam and across the base; turn right sides out. Repeat for the arms and tail.

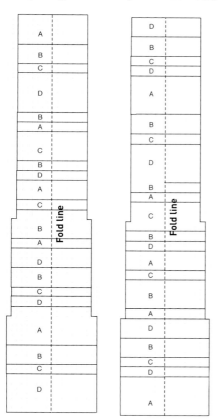

Right leg × 1

Left leg × 1

Fold line

Body: Sew the two body pieces together on both sides and across the bottom, catching the tops of the legs into the bottom seam. Leave the top open. Sew the patches to the front using large overcast stitches in a contrasting colour. Sew the cast-off row of each arm flat to the body on each side, placing the seam towards the front. Attach the tail in the same way to the bottom of the stripe in **D** on the back. Fill the body and gather the top.

Head: Sew the two head pieces together leaving an opening on one side. Embroider the nose at the tip in long satin stitch using **D**. For the eyes, place the white felt/fleece circles on to the orange circles and attach to the head using bold black stitches. Fill the head and close the opening.

Finishing: Place the head on the top of the body, overlapping the two pieces by 5cm (2in). Sew the top of the back to the back of the head. Secure the bottom of the head to the body with some invisible stitches.

BIG WOLF (continued)

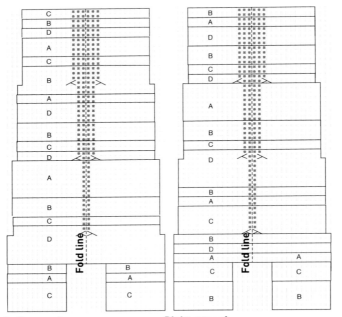

Left arm × 1

Right arm × 1

Body × 2

Leg

Leg

A = dark blue
B = lime green
C = red
D = deep pink
E = light grey

■ = decreased stitch (no stitch)
⟨ = k2tog
⟩ = sl1, k1, psso

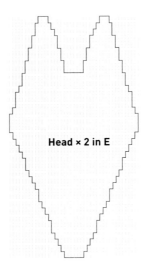

Head × 2 in E

25 LITTLE WOLF

SIZE: about 40cm (15¾in) high

MATERIALS

DK (sport) weight yarn (50% wool/50% acrylic): 1 ball each of dark blue (**A**), lime green (**B**), red (**C**) deep pink (**D**) and light grey (**E**)
Two circles of orange felt or polar fleece for the eyes
Black embroidery thread/yarn
Synthetic filling
2.5mm (US size 1) knitting needles or size needed to obtain tension (gauge)

STITCHES

Stocking stitch (st st): knit right-side rows; purl wrong-side rows.

TENSION (GAUGE)

30 sts and 40 rows in st st = 10cm (4in).

INSTRUCTIONS

Referring to the grid patterns, knit the following in st st:
In **E**: two heads.
In **A**, **B**, **C** and **D**: two bodies, one tail, one right leg, one left leg, one right arm and one left arm.
Make the decreases two stitches away from the edges.
Patches: For the large patch, cast on 12 sts in **E**. Knit 12 rows in plain st st and cast off.
For the small patch, cast on 10 sts in **E**. Knit 8 rows in plain st st and cast off.

ASSEMBLY

Legs, arms and tail: Fold each leg in half lengthways, with right sides facing. Stitch the side seam and across the base; turn right sides out. Repeat for the arms and tail.
Body: Sew the two body pieces together on both sides and across the bottom, catching the tops of the legs into the bottom seam. Leave the top open. Sew the patches to the front using large overcast stitches in a contrasting colour. Sew the cast-off row of each arm flat to the body on each side, placing the seam towards the front. Attach the tail in the same way to the bottom of the stripe in **D** on the back. Fill the body and gather the top.
Head: Sew the two head pieces together leaving an opening on one side. Embroider the nose at the tip in long satin stitch using **D**. For the eyes, place the orange felt/fleece circles on the head and attach them using bold black stitches. Fill the head and close the opening.
Finishing: Place the head on the top of the body, overlapping the two pieces by 5cm (2in). Sew the top of the back to the back of the head. Secure the bottom of the head to the body with some invisible stitches.

Tips

To personalize either of the wolves, simply embroider a child's initials on the top patch.
The lower patch can be turned into a handy pocket. Just attach it around the sides and base, leaving the top edge open.

LITTLE WOLF (continued)

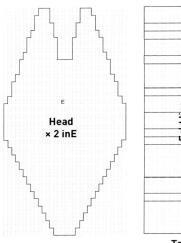

Head
× 2 in E

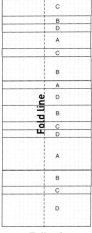

Tail × 1

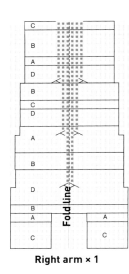

Right arm × 1

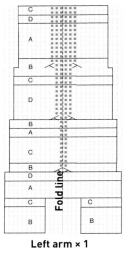

Left arm × 1

Right leg × 1   **Left leg × 1**

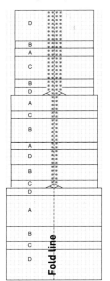

Body × 2

A = dark blue
B = lime green
C = red
D = deep pink
E = light grey

■ = decreased stitch (no stitch)
✕ = k2tog
✕ = sl1, k1, psso

26 DACHSHUND

SIZE: about 6.5cm (2½in) long

MATERIALS

DK (sport) weight yarn (50% wool/50% acrylic): 1 ball each of white (**A**) and orange (**B**)
Brown or black embroidery thread/yarn
Synthetic filling
1 swivel snap hook
1.75mm (US size 6) crochet hook

STITCHES

Foundation chain (ch), slip stitch (sl st) and US single crochet/UK double crochet (see page 64).

INSTRUCTIONS

Head

Using A, 3ch and join with sl st to form a ring.
Round 1: 1ch, 8sc (*UK dc*) into the ring, join with sl st into the ch at start of round [8 sts].
Round 2: 1ch, 2sc (*UK dc*) into each sc (*UK dc*), join with sl st into the ch at start of round [16 sts].
Rounds 3–7: 1ch, sc (*UK dc*) into each sc (*UK dc*), sl st into the ch at start of round.
Round 8: 1ch, *2sc (*UK dc*) into next sc (*UK dc*), 1sc (*UK dc*) into the following sc (*UK dc*)*; repeat from * to * all around, join with sl st into the ch at start of round [24 sts].
Round 9: 1ch, sc (*UK dc*) into each sc (*UK dc*), join with sl st into the ch at start of round.
Round 10: 1ch, * sc (*UK dc*) into each of the 2 following sc (*UK dc*), skip next sc (*UK dc*)*. Repeat from * to * all around, join with sl st into the ch at start of round [16 sts].

Rounds 11–12: as round 9. At the end of round 12, slip some filling into the shape.
Round 13: as round 10, sc (*UK dc*) into final stitch [11 sts].
Round 14: as round 9.
Rounds 15–16: 1ch, *sc (*UK dc*) into next sc (*UK dc*), skip the following sc (*UK dc*)*. Repeat from * to * all around, join with sl st into the ch at start of round [6 sts].
Break off the yarn, pass it into the remaining stitches and pull up to close the hole. Finish off.

Body

Using A, 3ch and join with sl st to form a ring.
Round 1: 1ch, 8sc (*UK dc*) into the ring, join with sl st into the ch at start of round [8 sts].
Round 2: 1ch, 2sc (*UK dc*) into each sc (*UK dc*), sl st into the ch at start of round [16 sts].
Round 3: 1ch, *2sc (*UK dc*) into next sc (*UK dc*), sc (*UK dc*) into the following sc (*UK dc*)*. Repeat from * to * all around, sl st into the ch at start of round [24 sts].
Rounds 4–15: 1 ch, sc (*UK dc*) into each sc (*UK dc*), sl st into the ch at start of round. At the end of round 15, slip some filling into the shape.
Round 16: 1 ch, *sc (*UK dc*) into each of the next 2 sc (*UK dc*), skip following sc (*UK dc*)*. Repeat from * to * all around, sl st into the ch at start of round [16 sts].
Rounds 17–18: 1 ch, *sc (*UK dc*) into next sc (*UK dc*), skip the following sc (*UK dc*)*. Repeat from * to * all around, sl st into the ch at start of round [4 sts].
Break off the yarn, pass it into the remaining stitches and pull up to close the hole. Finish off.

DACHSHUND (continued)

Ears (× 2)
Using **B**, 3ch.
Row 1: 1ch (turning chain) 3sc (*UK dc*).
Row 2: 1ch, 2sc (*UK dc*) into the next sc (*UK dc*), 1sc (*UK dc*), 2sc (*UK dc*) into the last sc (*UK dc*) [5 sts].
Row 3: 1ch, 2sc (*UK dc*) into the next sc (*UK dc*), sc (*UK dc*) into each of the next 3 sc (*UK dc*), 2sc (*UK dc*) into the last sc (*UK dc*) [7 sts].
Rows 4–9: 1ch, sc (*UK dc*) into each sc (*UK dc*). Finish off.

Tail
Join yarn **B** to the top-back end of the body with sl st. Crochet 8ch (this includes a turning chain).
Row 1: 7sc (*UK dc*).
Row 2: 1ch, sc (*UK dc*) into each of the next 2 sc (*UK dc*), sl st into the following sc (*UK dc*). Fasten off.

Legs (× 4)
Using **B**, 3ch. Join with sl st to form a ring.
Row 1: 1ch, 8sc (*UK dc*) into the ring, join with sl st into the ch at start of round [8 sts].
Rows 2–4: 1ch, sc (*UK dc*) into each sc (*UK dc*). Trim off the yarn and slip some filling into the shape.

ASSEMBLY

Facial features: Embroider the nose in satin stitch using **B**. Embroider each eye with a single long stitch in brown or black. Use the same colour to mark the mouth with a line of backstitches.
Joining: Sew an ear to each side of the head. Attach the legs to the body. Sew the head to the body.
Snap hook: Join yarn **A** to the back of the head with sl st; 5ch, sl st into the previous stitch, passing through the snap hook, then 5ch and sl st into the head just next to the first stitch. Finish off.

27 CHIHUAHUA

SIZE: about 6.5cm (2½in) long

MATERIALS

DK (sport) weight yarn (50% wool/50% acrylic): 1 ball each of white (**A**) and light grey (**B**)
Black embroidery thread/yarn
Synthetic filling
1 swivel snap hook
1.75mm (US size 6) crochet hook

STITCHES

Foundation chain (ch), slip stitch (sl st) and US single crochet/UK double crochet (see page 64).

INSTRUCTIONS

Head
Using **A**, 3ch and join with sl st to form a ring.
Round 1: 1ch, 8sc (*UK dc*) into the ring, join with sl st into the ch at start of round [8 sts].
Round 2: 1ch, 2sc (*UK dc*) into each sc (*UK dc*), sl st into the ch at start of round [16 sts].
Round 3: 1ch, *2sc (*UK dc*) into the next sc (*UK dc*), 1sc (*UK dc*) into the following sc (*UK dc*)*. Repeat from * to * all around, sl st into the ch at start of round [24 sts].
Round 4: 1ch, *2sc (*UK dc*) into the next sc (*UK dc*), 1sc (*UK dc*) into each of the following 2sc (*UK dc*)*. Repeat from * to * all around, sl st into the ch at start of round [32 sts].
Rounds 5–13: 1ch, 1sc (*UK dc*) into each sc (*UK dc*), sl st into the ch at start of round. At the end of round 13, slip some filling into the shape.

Round 14: 1ch, *1sc (*UK dc*) into the 3 next sc (*UK dc*), skip the following sc (*UK dc*)*. Repeat from * to * all around, sl st into the ch at start of round [24 sts].

Round 15: 1ch, *1sc (*UK dc*) into the 2 next sc (*UK dc*), skip the following sc (*UK dc*)*. Repeat from * to * all around, sl st into the ch at start of round [16 sts].

Rounds 16–17: 1ch, *1sc (*UK dc*) into the next sc (*UK dc*), skip the following sc (*UK dc*)*. Repeat from * to * all around, sl st into the ch at start of round [4 sts].

Break off the yarn, pass it into the remaining stitches and pull up to close the hole. Finish off.

Body

Using **A**, 3ch and join with sl st to form a ring.

Round 1: 1ch, 8sc (*UK dc*) into the ring, sl st into the ch at start of round [8 sts].

Round 2: 1ch, 2sc (*UK dc*) into each sc (*UK dc*), sl st into the ch at start of round [16 sts].

Round 3: 1ch, *2sc (*UK dc*) into the next sc (*UK dc*), 1sc (*UK dc*) into the following sc (*UK dc*)*. Repeat from * to * all around, sl st into the ch at start of round [24 sts].

Rounds 4–10: 1ch, 1sc (*UK dc*) into each sc (*UK dc*), sl st into the ch at start of round. At the end of round 10, slip some filling into the shape.

Round 11: 1ch, *1sc (*UK dc*) into each of the next 2 sc (*UK dc*), skip the following sc (*UK dc*)*. Repeat from * to * all around, sl st into the ch at start of round [16 sts].

Rounds 12–13: 1ch, *1sc (*UK dc*) into the next sc (*UK dc*), skip the following sc (*UK dc*)*. Repeat from * to * all around, sl st into the ch at start of round [4 sts].

Break off the yarn, pass it into the remaining stitches and pull up to close the hole. Finish off.

Legs (× 4)

Using **A**, 6ch.

Rows 1–6: 1ch, 1sc (*UK dc*) into each of the 6sc (*UK dc*).

Row 7: to make the foot, 1ch, 2sc (*UK dc*) into the first sc, sc into each of next 4 sc (*UK dc*), 2sc (*UK dc*) into the last sc (*UK dc*) [8 sts].

Row 8: 1ch, 2sc (*UK dc*) into the first sc (*UK dc*), sc (*UK dc*) into each of next 6 sc (*UK dc*), 2sc (*UK dc*) into the last sc (*UK dc*) [10 sts]. Break off the yarn, leaving a tail to stitch the seam. Fold each leg in half lengthways and join the long edges. Finish off neatly.

Muzzle

Using **A**, 3ch. Join with sl st to make a ring.

Round 1: 1ch, 8sc (*UK dc*) into the ring, join with sl st into the ch at start of round [8 sts].

Round 2: 1ch, 2sc (*UK dc*) into each sc (*UK dc*), join with sl st into the ch at start of round [16 sts]. Finish off.

Eyes (× 2)

Using **A**, 3ch. Join with sl st to make a ring.

Round 1: 1ch, 6sc (*UK dc*) into the ring, join with sl st into the ch at start of round. Finish off.

Ears (× 2)

Using **B**, 5ch.

Row 1: 1ch, sc (*UK dc*) into each sc (*UK dc*) [5 sts].

Row 2: 1ch, skip the first sc (*UK dc*), sc (*UK dc*) into each sc (*UK dc*) [4 sts].

Row 3: 1ch, skip the first sc (*UK dc*), sc (*UK dc*) into each sc (*UK dc*) [3 sts].

Row 4: 1ch, skip the first sc (*UK dc*), sc (*UK dc*) into each sc (*UK dc*) [2 sts].

Row 5: 1ch, skip the first sc (*UK dc*), sc (*UK dc*) into remaining sc (*UK dc*) [1 st]. Finish off.

CHIHUAHUA (continued)

ASSEMBLY

Face: Sew the muzzle on to the front of the head using backstitch. Sew the eyes above the muzzle. Using black thread, embroider a French knot in the centre of each eye; use satin stitch for the nose and mouth.
Ears: Sew the widest part of the ears to the top of the head.
Legs and head: Sew two legs to the front of the body and the other two to each side so that the dog is sitting. Attach the head to the body.
Tail: For the tail, join yarn **B** to the base of the back with sl st; 7ch (includes turning chain). Sl st into each ch [6 sts] then join to the body with sl st. Finish off.
Snap hook: Join yarn **A** to the head with sl st; 5ch, sl st into the previous stitch, passing through the snap hook, then 5ch and sl st into the head just next to the first stitch. Finish off.

28 HEDGEHOG

SIZE: about 6.5cm (2½in) high

MATERIALS

DK (sport) weight yarn (50% wool/50% acrylic): 1 ball each of dark brown (**A**) and light brown (**B**)
Synthetic filling
1 swivel snap hook
1.75mm (US size 6) crochet hook

STITCHES

Foundation chain (ch), slip stitch (sl st) and US single crochet/UK double crochet (see page 64).

INSTRUCTIONS

Body
Using **B**, 3ch and join with sl st into a ring.
Round 1: 1ch, 8sc (*UK dc*) into the ring, sl st into the ch at start of round [8 sts].
Round 2: 1ch, 2sc (*UK dc*) into each sc (*UK dc*), sl st into the ch at start of round [16 sts].
Round 3: 1ch, *2sc (*UK dc*) into the next sc (*UK dc*), 1sc (*UK dc*) into the following sc (*UK dc*)*. Repeat from * to * all around, sl st into the ch at start of round [24 sts].
Round 4: 1ch, *2sc (*UK dc*) into the next sc (*UK dc*), sc (*UK dc*) into each of the following 2 sc (*UK dc*)*. Repeat from * to * all around, sl st into the ch at start of round [32 sts].
Rounds 5–11: 1ch, sc (*UK dc*) into each sc (*UK dc*), sl st into the ch at start of round.

Round 12: 1ch, *1sc (*UK dc*) into each of the next 3 sc (*UK dc*), skip the following sc (*UK dc*)*. Repeat from * to * all around, sl st into the ch at start of round [24 sts]. At the end of the round, slip some filling into the shape.

Round 13: 1ch, *1sc (*UK dc*) into each of the next 2 sc (*UK dc*), skip the following sc (*UK dc*)*. Repeat from * to * all around, sl st into the ch at start of round [16 sts].

Rounds 14–15: 1ch, * 1sc (*UK dc*) into the next sc (*UK dc*), skip the following sc (*UK dc*)*. Repeat from * to * all round, sl st into the ch at start of round [4 sts].

Break off the yarn, pass it into the remaining stitches and pull up to close the hole. Finish off.

Muzzle

Using **B**, 3ch and join with sl st into a ring.

Round 1: 1ch, 8sc (*UK dc*) into the ring, sl st into the ch at start of round [8 sts].

Rounds 2–5: 1ch, sc (*UK dc*) into each sc (*UK dc*), sl st into the ch at start of round.

Round 6: 1ch, *1sc (*UK dc*) into each of the next 2 sc (*UK dc*), skip the following sc (*UK dc*)*. Repeat from * to * all around, sl st into the ch at start of round [6 sts]. Finish off.

Legs (× 4)

Using **A**, 3ch and join with sl st into a ring.

Round 1: 1ch, 8sc (*UK dc*) into the ring, sl st into the ch at start of round [8 sts].

Rounds 2–4: 1ch, 1sc (*UK dc*) into each sc (*UK dc*). Break off the yarn and slip some filling into the shape.

ASSEMBLY

Face: Stuff the muzzle and sew it on to the front of the body, leaving space below for the legs. Embroider the eyes and the nose in yarn **A**.

Legs: Sew the legs on to the front of the body.

Spines: Wrap yarn **A** around a piece of card 10cm (4in) long. Cut one end then tie the threads to the back of the hedgehog with the help of a crochet hook to make the spines.

Snap hook: Join yarn **A** to the top of the head with sl st; 5ch, sl st into the previous stitch, passing through the snap hook, then 5ch and sl st into the head just next to the first stitch. Finish off.

CROCHETED
ANIMAL
CHARMS

29 SQUIRREL

SIZE: about 6.5cm (2½in) long

MATERIALS

4-ply (fingering) weight yarn (30% lambswool/70% acrylic): 1 ball of light brown (**A**)
DK (sport) weight yarn (50% wool/50% acrylic): 1 ball of orange (**B**)
Aran (worsted) weight eyelash yarn: 1 ball copper (**C**)
Synthetic filling
1 swivel snap hook
1.75mm (US size 6) and 2mm (US size 4) crochet hooks

STITCHES

Foundation chain (ch), slip stitch (sl st) and US single crochet/UK double crochet (see page 64).

INSTRUCTIONS

Head
Using **A** and the 1.75mm crochet hook (US size 6), 3ch and join with sl st into a ring.
Round 1: 1ch, 8sc (*UK dc*) into the ring, sl st into the ch at start of round [8 sts].
Round 2: 1ch, 2sc (*UK dc*) into each sc (*UK dc*), sl st into the ch at start of round [16 sts].
Round 3: 1ch, *2sc (*UK dc*) into the next sc (*UK dc*), 1sc (*UK dc*) into the following sc (*UK dc*)*. Repeat from * to * all around, sl st into the ch at start of round [24 sts].
Round 4: 1ch, *2sc (*UK dc*) into the next sc (*UK dc*), sc (*UK dc*) into each of the following 2 sc (*UK dc*)*. Repeat from * to * all around, sl st into the ch at start of round [32 sts].
Rounds 5–10: 1ch, sc (*UK dc*) into each sc (*UK dc*), sl st into the ch at start of round. At the end of round 10, slip some filling into the shape.
Round 11: 1ch, *1sc (*UK dc*) into the next 3 sc (*UK dc*), skip the following sc (*UK dc*)*. Repeat from * to * all around, sl st into the ch at start of round [24 sts].
Round 12: 1ch, *1sc (*UK dc*) into each of the next 2 sc (*UK dc*), skip the following sc (*UK dc*)*. Repeat from * to * all around, sl st into the ch at start of round [16 sts].
Rounds 13–14: 1ch, *1sc (*UK dc*) into the next sc (*UK dc*), skip the following sc (*UK dc*)*. Repeat from * to * all around, sl st into the ch at start of round [4 sts].
Break off the yarn, pass it into the remaining stitches and pull up to close the hole. Finish off.

Body

Using **A** and the 1.75mm (US size 6) crochet hook, 3ch and join with sl st into a ring.

Round 1: 1ch, 8sc (*UK dc*) into the ring, sl st into the ch at start of round [8 sts].

Round 2: 1ch, 2sc (*UK dc*) into each sc (*UK dc*), sl st into the ch at start of round [16 sts].

Round 3: 1ch, *2sc (*UK dc*) into next sc (*UK dc*), 1sc (*UK dc*) into the following sc (*UK dc*)*. Repeat from * to * all around, sl st into the ch at start of round [24 sts].

Rounds 4–9: 1ch, 1sc (*UK dc*) into each sc (*UK dc*), sl st into the ch at start of round.

Round 10: 1ch, *1sc (*UK dc*) into each of the next 3 sc (*UK dc*), skip the following sc (*UK dc*)*. Repeat from * to * all around, sl st into the ch at start of round [18 sts]. At the end of the round, slip some filling into the shape.

Round 11: 1ch, *1sc (*UK dc*) into the next 2 sc (*UK dc*), skip the following sc (*UK dc*)*. Repeat from * to * all around, sl st into the ch at start of round [12 sts].

Rounds 12–13: 1ch, *1sc (*UK dc*) into the next sc (*UK dc*), skip the following sc (*UK dc*)*. Repeat from * to * all around, sl st into the ch at start of round [3 sts].

Break off the yarn, pass it into the remaining stitches and pull up to close the hole. Finish off.

Legs (× 4)

Using **A** and the 1.75mm (US size 6) crochet hook, 3ch and join with sl st into a ring.

Round 1: 1ch, 8sc (*UK dc*) into the ring, sl st into the ch at start of round [8 sts].

Rounds 2–4: 1ch, 1sc (*UK dc*) into each sc (*UK dc*). Break off the yarn and slip some filling into the shape.

Nose

Using **B** and the 1.75mm (US size 6) crochet hook, 3ch and join with sl st into a ring.

Round 1: 1ch, 8sc (*UK dc*) into the ring, sl st into the ch at start of round [8 sts].

Round 2: 1ch, 2sc (*UK dc*) into each sc (*UK dc*), sl st into the ch at start of round [16 sts]. Finish off.

Ears (× 2)

Using **B** and the 1.75mm (US size 6) crochet hook, 5ch.

Round 1: 1ch, sc (*UK dc*) into each sc (*UK dc*) [5 sts].

Round 2: 1ch, skip the first sc (*UK dc*), sc (*UK dc*) into each sc (*UK dc*) [4 sts].

Round 3: 1ch, skip the first sc (*UK dc*), sc (*UK dc*) into each sc (*UK dc*) [3 sts].

Round 4: 1 ch, skip the first sc (*UK dc*), sc (*UK dc*) into each sc (*UK dc*) [2 sts].

Round 5: 1ch, skip the first sc (*UK dc*), sc (*UK dc*) into the remaining sc (*UK dc*) [1 st]. Finish off.

Tail

Using **C** and the 2mm (US size 4) crochet hook, 8ch (includes turning ch).

Row 1: 7sc (*UK dc*) [7 sts].

Row 2: 1ch, 2sc (*UK dc*) into the first sc (*UK dc*), sc (*UK dc*) into each of the next 5 sc (*UK dc*), 2sc (*UK dc*) into the last sc (*UK dc*) [9 sts].

Row 3: ch, 2sc (*UK dc*) into the first sc (*UK dc*), sc (*UK dc*) into each of the next 7 sc (*UK dc*), 2sc (*UK dc*) into the last sc (*UK dc*) [11 sts].

Rows 4–9: 1ch to turn then sc (*UK dc*) into each sc (*UK dc*).

Row 10: 1ch, skip the first sc (*UK dc*), sc (*UK dc*) into each of the next 9 sc (*UK dc*) and turn without working into the final sc (*UK dc*) [9 sts].

Row 11: 1ch, skip the first sc (*UK dc*), sc (*UK dc*) into each of the next 7 sc (*UK dc*); turn [7 sts].

Row 12: 1ch, skip the first sc (*UK dc*), sc (*UK dc*) into each of the next 5 sc (*UK dc*), leaving the final sc (*UK dc*) unworked [5 sts]. Break off yarn, leaving a length to stitch the seam. Fold the knitted piece in half and join the side edges.

ASSEMBLY

Joining the parts: Sew the nose and the ears to the head. Attach the legs to the front of the body. Now attach the head. Sew the tail flat on to the back and the rear of the head (see photograph).

Snap hook: Join yarn **A** to the top of the head with sl st; 5ch, sl st into the previous stitch, passing through the snap hook, then 5ch and sl st into the head just next to the first stitch. Finish off.

30 SHEEP

SIZE: about 6.5cm (2½in) high

MATERIALS

DK (sport) weight yarn (50% wool/50% acrylic): 1 ball each of pale pink (**A**) and white (**B**)
Black embroidery thread/yarn
Synthetic filling
1 swivel snap hook
1.75mm (US size 6) crochet hook

STITCHES

Foundation chain (ch), slip stitch (sl st) and US single crochet/UK double crochet (see page 64).

INSTRUCTIONS

Head

Using **B**, 3ch and join with sl st into a ring.
Round 1: 1ch, 8sc (*UK dc*) into the ring, sl st into the ch at start of round [8 sts].
Round 2: 1ch, 2sc (*UK dc*) into each sc (*UK dc*), sl st into the ch at start of round [16 sts].
Round 3: 1ch, *2sc (*UK dc*) into the next sc (*UK dc*), sc (*UK dc*) into the following sc (*UK dc*)*. Repeat from * to * all around, sl st into the ch at start of round [24 sts].
Round 4: 1ch, *2sc (*UK dc*) into the next sc (*UK dc*), 1sc (*UK dc*) into the following 2 sc (*UK dc*)*. Repeat from * to * all around, sl st into the ch at start of round [32 sts].
Round 5: 1ch, * 2sc (*UK dc*) into the next sc (*UK dc*), 1sc (*UK dc*) into the following 3 sc (*UK dc*)*. Repeat from * to * all around, sl st into the ch at start of round [40 sts].

Rounds 6–9: 1ch, 1sc (*UK dc*) into each sc (*UK dc*), sl st into the ch at start of round.
Round 10: 1ch, *1sc (*UK dc*) into each of the next 3 sc (*UK dc*), skip the following sc (*UK dc*)*. Repeat from * to * all around, sl st into the ch at start of round [30 sts]. At the end of the round, slip some filling into the shape.
Round 11: 1ch, *1sc (*UK dc*) into the next 2 sc (*UK dc*), skip the following sc (*UK dc*)*. Repeat from * to * all around, sl st into the ch at start of round [20 sts].
Round 12: 1ch, * 1sc (*UK dc*) into the next sc (*UK dc*), skip the following sc (*UK dc*)*. Repeat from * to * all around, sl st into the ch at start of round [10 sts].
Break off the yarn, pass it into the remaining stitches and pull up to close the hole. Finish off (neck end).

Face

Using **A**, repeat rounds 1–3 for the head; finish off.

Ears (× 2)

Join yarn **A** to the side of the head, at eye level, using sl st, 7ch and sl st into the head next to the first sl st; finish off.

Body

Using **B**, 3ch and join with sl st into a ring.
Round 1: 1ch, 8sc (*UK dc*) into the ring, sl st into the ch at start of round [8 sts].
Round 2: 1ch, 2sc (*UK dc*) into each sc (*UK dc*), sl st into the ch at start of round [16 sts].
Round 3: 1ch, *2sc (*UK dc*) into the next sc (*UK dc*), 1sc (*UK dc*) into the following sc (*UK dc*)*. Repeat from * to * all around, sl st into the ch at start of round [24 sts].

Round 4: 1ch, *2sc (*UK dc*) into the next sc (*UK dc*), 1sc (*UK dc*) into each of the following 2 sc (*UK dc*)*. Repeat from * to * all around, sl st into the ch at start of round [32 sts].

Round 5: 1ch, *2sc (*UK dc*) into the next sc (*UK dc*), 1sc (*UK dc*) into each of the following 3 sc (*UK dc*)*. Repeat from * to * all around, sl st into the ch at start of round [40 sts].

Rounds 6–12: 1ch, 1sc (*UK dc*) into each sc (*UK dc*), sl st into the ch at start of round.

Round 13: 1ch, * 1sc (*UK dc*) into the next 3 sc (*UK dc*), skip the following sc (*UK dc*)*. Repeat from * to * all around, sl st into the ch at start of round [30 sts]. At the end of the round, slip some filling into the shape.

Round 14: 1ch, * 1sc (*UK dc*) into each of the next 2 sc (*UK dc*), skip the following sc (*UK dc*)*. Repeat from * to * all around, sl st into the ch at start of round [20 sts].

Round 15: 1ch, * 1sc (*UK dc*) into the next sc (*UK dc*), skip the following sc (*UK dc*)*. Repeat from * to * all around, 1 sl st into the ch at start of round [10 sts].
Break off the yarn, pass it into the remaining stitches and pull up to close the hole.

Legs (× 4)
Using **B**, 3ch and join with sl st into a ring.

Round 1: 1ch, 8sc (*UK dc*) into the ring, sl st into the ch at start of round [8 sts].

Round 2: 1ch, 2sc (*UK dc*) into each sc (*UK dc*), sl st into the ch at start of round [16 sts].

Rounds 3–6: 1ch, 1sc (*UK dc*) into each sc (*UK dc*), sl st into the ch at start of round. Break off the yarn and slip some filling into the shape.

ASSEMBLY

Face: Sew the face to the head using backstitch. Embroider the eyes, mouth and nose in black using straight stitches.

Joining the parts: Sew the legs to the front of the body so that the sheep is sitting down. Sew the head to the top of the body.

Snap hook: Join yarn **B** to the top of the head with sl st; 5ch, sl st into the previous stitch, passing through the snap hook, then 5ch and sl st into the head just next to the first stitch. Finish off.

Tip

You'll have plenty of pink yarn left over at the end of this project. Put it to good use by making the pig on page 118.

CROCHETED
ANIMAL
CHARMS

31 PIG

SIZE: about 6.5cm (2½in) high

MATERIALS

DK (sport) weight yarn (50% wool/50% acrylic): 1 ball of pale pink
Black embroidery thread/yarn
Synthetic filling
1 swivel snap hook
1.75mm (US size 6) crochet hook

STITCHES

Foundation chain (ch), slip stitch (sl st) and US single crochet/UK double crochet (see page 64).

INSTRUCTIONS

Head

Using your yarn, 3ch and join with sl st into a ring.
Round 1: 1ch, 8sc (*UK dc*) into the ring, sl st into the ch at start of round [8 sts].
Rounds 2–3: 1ch, 1sc (*UK dc*) into each sc (*UK dc*), sl st into the ch at start of round.
Round 4: 1ch, 2sc (*UK dc*) into each sc (*UK dc*), sl st into the ch at start of round [16 sts].
Round 5: 1ch, *2sc (*UK dc*) into the next sc (*UK dc*), 1sc (*UK dc*) into the following sc (*UK dc*)*. Repeat from * to * all around, sl st into the ch at start of round [24 sts].
Round 6: 1ch, *2sc (*UK dc*) into the next sc (*UK dc*), 1sc (*UK dc*) into each of the following 2 sc (*UK dc*)*. Repeat from * to * all around, sl st into the ch at start of round [32 sts].
Rounds 7–10: 1ch, 1sc (*UK dc*) into each sc (*UK dc*), sl st into the ch at start of round.
Round 11: 1ch, *1sc (*UK dc*) into each of the next 3 sc (*UK dc*), skip the following sc (*UK dc*)*. Repeat from * to * all around, sl st into the ch at start of round [24 sts]. Slip some filling into the shape.
Round 12: 1ch, *1sc (*UK dc*) into each of the next 2 sc (*UK dc*), skip the following sc (*UK dc*)*. Repeat from * to * all around, sl st into the ch at start of round [16 sts].
Round 13: 1ch, *1sc (*UK dc*) into the next sc (*UK dc*), skip the following sc (*UK dc*)*. Repeat from * to * all around, sl st into the ch at start of round [8 sts].
Break off the yarn, pass it into the remaining stitches and pull up to close the hole.

Body

Using your yarn, 3ch and join with sl st into a ring.

Round 1: 1ch, 8sc (*UK dc*) into the ring, sl st into the ch at start of round [8 sts].

Round 2: 1ch, 2sc (*UK dc*) into each sc (*UK dc*), sl st into the ch at the start of round [16 sts].

Round 3: 1ch, *2sc (*UK dc*) into the next sc (*UK dc*), 1sc (*UK dc*) into the following sc (*UK dc*)*. Repeat from * to * all around, sl st into the ch at start of round [24 sts].

Round 4: 1ch, *2sc (*UK dc*) into the next sc (*UK dc*), 1sc (*UK dc*) into each of the following 2 sc (*UK dc*)*. Repeat from * to * all around, sl st into the ch at start of round [32 sts].

Rounds 5–10: 1ch, 1sc (*UK dc*) into each sc (*UK dc*), sl st into the ch at start of round.

Round 11: 1ch, *1sc (*UK dc*) into each of the next 3 sc (*UK dc*), skip the following sc (*UK dc*)*. Repeat from * to * all around, sl st into the ch at start of round [24 sts]. Slip some filling into the shape.

Round 12: 1ch, *1sc (*UK dc*) into each of the next 2 sc (*UK dc*), skip the following sc (*UK dc*)*. Repeat from * to * all around, sl st into the ch at start of round [16 sts].

Round 13: 1ch, *1sc (*UK dc*) into the next sc (*UK dc*), skip the following sc (*UK dc*)*. Repeat from * to * all around, sl st into the ch at start of round [8 sts].

Break off the yarn, pass it into the remaining stitches and pull up to close the hole at the neck; finish off.

Tail

Join the yarn to the body in the appropriate position using sl st, 6ch (includes turning chain). Return in sc (*UK dc*) and finish off using sl st on to the first stitch.

Ears (× 2)

Using your yarn 3ch.

Rows 1–2: 1ch, 1sc (*UK dc*) into each sc (*UK dc*) [3 sts].

Row 3: 1ch, skip first sc (*UK dc*), 1sc (*UK dc*) into each sc (*UK dc*) [2 sts].

Row 4: 1ch, skip first sc (*UK dc*), 1sc (*UK dc*); finish off.

Legs (× 4)

Using your yarn, 3ch and join with sl st into a ring.

Round 1: 1ch, 8sc (*UK dc*) into the ring, sl st into the ch at start of round [8 sts].

Round 2: 1ch, 2sc (*UK dc*) into each sc (*UK dc*), sl st into the ch at start of round [16 sts].

Rounds 3–6: 1ch, 1sc (*UK dc*) into each sc (*UK dc*), sl st into the ch at start of round; finish off. Slip some filling into the shape.

ASSEMBLY

Joining the parts: Sew the legs underneath the body. Sew the head on to the body then sew the ears on to the head.

Eyes: Embroider a French knot in black for each eye.

Snap hook: Join the yarn to the back with sl st; 5ch, sl st into the previous stitch, passing through the snap hook, then 5ch and sl st into the back just next to the first stitch. Finish off.

CROCHETED
ANIMAL
CHARMS

32 COW

SIZE: about 6.5cm (2½in) high

MATERIALS

DK (sport) weight yarn (50% wool/50% acrylic): 1 ball each of white (**A**) and black (**B**)
Synthetic filling
1 swivel snap hook
1.75mm (US size 6) crochet hook

STITCHES

Foundation chain (ch); slip stitch (sl st); US single crochet/UK double crochet; US half double crochet/UK half treble; and US double crochet/UK treble crochet (see page 64).

INSTRUCTIONS

Head

Using **A**, 3ch and join with sl st into a ring.
Round 1: 1ch, 8sc (*UK dc*) into the ring, sl st into the ch at start of round [8 sts].
Round 2: 1ch, 2sc (*UK dc*) into each sc (*UK dc*), sl st into the ch at start of round [16 sts].
Round 3: 1ch, *2sc (*UK dc*) into the next sc (*UK dc*), 1sc (*UK dc*) into the following sc (*UK dc*)*. Repeat from * to * all around, sl st into the ch at start of round [24 sts].
Rounds 4–9: 1ch, 1sc (*UK dc*) into each sc (*UK dc*), sl st into the ch at start of round.
Round 10: 1ch, *1sc (*UK dc*) into each of the next 3 sc (*UK dc*), skip the following sc (*UK dc*)*. Repeat from * to * all around, sl st into the ch at start of round [18 sts].
Rounds 11–16: 1ch, 1sc (*UK dc*) into each sc (*UK dc*), sl st into the ch at start of round. At the end of round 16, slip some filling into the shape.
Round 17: 1ch, *1sc (*UK dc*) into each of the next 2 sc (*UK dc*), skip the following sc (*UK dc*)*. Repeat from * to * all around, sl st into the ch at start of round [12 sts].
Round 18: 1ch, *1sc (*UK dc*) into the next sc (*UK dc*), skip the following sc (*UK dc*)*. Repeat from * to * all around, sl st into the ch at start of round [6 sts].
Break off the yarn, pass it into the remaining stitches and pull up to close the hole. Finish off.

Body

Using **A**, 3ch and join with sl st into a ring.

Round 1: 1ch, 8sc (*UK dc*) into the ring, sl st into the ch at start of round [8 sts].

Round 2: 1ch, 2sc (*UK dc*) into each sc (*UK dc*), sl st into the ch at start of round [16 sts].

Round 3: 1ch, *2sc (*UK dc*) into the next sc (*UK dc*), 1sc (*UK dc*) into the following sc (*UK dc*)*. Repeat from * to * all around, sl st into the ch at start of round [24 sts].

Rounds 4–9: 1ch, 1sc (*UK dc*) into each sc (*UK dc*), sl st into the ch at start of round.

Round 10: 1ch, *1sc (*UK dc*) into each of the next 3 sc (*UK dc*), skip the following sc (*UK dc*)*. Repeat from * to * all around, sl st into the ch at start of round [18 sts]. At the end of the round, slip some filling into the shape.

Round 11: 1ch, *1sc (*UK dc*) into each of the next 2 sc (*UK dc*), skip the following sc (*UK dc*)*. Repeat from * to * all around, sl st into the ch at start of round [12 sts].

Round 12: 1ch, *1sc (*UK dc*) into the next sc (*UK dc*), skip the following sc (*UK dc*)*. Repeat from * to * all around, sl st into the ch at start of round [6 sts].

Break off the yarn, pass it into the remaining stitches and pull up to close the hole. Finish off.

Legs

Using **A**, 3ch and join with sl st into a ring.

Round 1: 1ch, 8sc (*UK dc*) into the ring, sl st into the ch at start of round [8 sts].

Rounds 2–4: 1ch, 1sc (*UK dc*) into each sc (*UK dc*).

Break off the yarn and slip some filling into the shape. Repeat to make a total of three legs in **A** and one in **B**.

Muzzle

This is worked in an oval shape around a foundation chain. Using **A**, 7ch (includes turning chain).

Round 1: sc (*UK dc*) into each of the first 5 ch, 3sc (*UK dc*) into the last ch; then work back down the other side of the foundation chain with 1sc (*UK dc*) into each of the first 5 ch, 2sc (*UK dc*) into the last ch, sl st into the ch at start of row.

Rounds 2–3: 1ch, 1sc (*UK dc*) into each sc (*UK dc*) on this edge, 3sc (*UK dc*) into the centre sc (*UK dc*) of the 3sc (*UK dc*) of the previous round, 1sc (*UK dc*) into each sc (*UK dc*) of the other edge and 2sc (*UK dc*) into the last sc (*UK dc*), sl st into the ch at start of round. Break off the yarn.

Ears (× 2)

Join yarn **B** to the side of the head, at eye level, using sl st, 7ch and sl st next to the first sl st; finish off.

Horns (× 2)

Using **A**, 4ch.

Row 1: 1ch, 1sc (*UK dc*), 1hdc (*UK htr*), 2dc (*UK tr*); finish off.

ASSEMBLY

Head: Sew the muzzle on to the head using backstitch. Attach the base of the horns to the top of the head, between the ears.

Facial features: Using **B**, embroider the mouth using backstitch, the nostrils and eye patch with satin stitch and one eye with a French knot; use **A** to embroider the other eye with a French knot on the eye patch.

Joining the parts: Attach the legs to the front of the body so that the cow is sitting down. Join the head to the body.

Marking: Embroider a 'splodge' in **B** on the side of the stomach using satin stitch.

Tail: Join yarn **B** to the bottom of the back with sl st, 9ch (includes turning ch). Return in sc (*UK dc*) then sl st next to the first sl st; finish off.

Snap hook: Join yarn **B** to the top of the head with sl st; 5ch, sl st into the previous stitch, passing through the snap hook, then 5ch and sl st into the head just next to the first stitch. Finish off.

33 BEAR

SIZE: about 6.5cm (2½in) high

MATERIALS

DK (sport) weight yarn (50% wool/50% acrylic): 1 ball of dark brown (**A**) and a small amount of orange (**B**)
4-ply (fingering) weight yarn (30% lambswool/70% acrylic): 1 ball of light brown (**C**)
Synthetic filling
1 swivel snap hook
1.75mm (US size 6) crochet hook

STITCHES

Foundation chain (ch); slip stitch (sl st); US single crochet/ UK double crochet, and US reverse single crochet/UK reverse double crochet (see page 64).

INSTRUCTIONS

Head
Using **C**, 3ch and join with sl st into a ring.
Round 1: 1ch, 8sc (*UK dc*) into the ring, sl st into the ch at start of round [8 sts].
Round 2: 1ch, 2sc (*UK dc*) into each sc (*UK dc*), sl st into the ch at start of round [16 sts].
Round 3: 1ch, *2sc (*UK dc*) into the next sc (*UK dc*), 1sc (*UK dc*) into the following sc (*UK dc*)*. Repeat from * to * all around, sl st into the ch at start of round [24 sts].
Round 4: 1ch, *2sc (*UK dc*) into the next sc (*UK dc*), 1sc (*UK dc*) into each of the following 2 sc (*UK dc*)*. Repeat from * to * all around, sl st into the ch at start of round [32 sts].
Round 5: 1ch, *2sc (*UK dc*) into the next sc (*UK dc*), 1sc (*UK dc*) into each of the following 3 sc (*UK dc*)*. Repeat from * to * all around, sl st into the ch at start of round [40 sts].
Rounds 6–9: 1ch, 1sc (*UK dc*) into each sc (*UK dc*), sl st into the ch at start of round.
Round 10: 1ch, *1sc (*UK dc*) into each of the next 3 sc (*UK dc*), skip following sc (*UK dc*)*. Repeat from * to * all around, sl st into the ch at start of round [30 sts]. At the end of the round, slip some filling into the shape.
Round 11: 1ch, * 1sc (*UK dc*) into the each of the next 2 sc (*UK dc*), skip the following sc (*UK dc*)*. Repeat from * to * all around, sl st into the ch at start of round [20 sts].
Round 12: 1ch, *1sc (*UK dc*) into the next sc (*UK dc*), skip the following sc (*UK dc*) *. Repeat from * to * all around, sl st into the ch at start of round [10 sts].
Break off the yarn, pass it into the remaining stitches and pull up to close the hole at the neck. Finish off.

Body

Using **C**, 3ch and join with sl st into a ring.

Round 1: 1ch, 8sc (*UK dc*) into the ring, sl st into the ch at start of round [8 sts].

Round 2: 1ch, 2sc (*UK dc*) into each sc (*UK dc*), sl st into the ch at start of round [16 sts].

Round 3: 1ch, *2sc (*UK dc*) into next sc (*UK dc*), 1sc (*UK dc*) into the following sc (*UK dc*)*. Repeat from * to * all around, sl st into the ch at start of round [24 sts].

Round 4: 1ch, *2sc (*UK dc*) into the next sc (*UK dc*), 1sc (*UK dc*) into each of the following 2 sc (*UK dc*)*. Repeat from * to * all around, sl st into the ch at start of round [32 sts].

Round 5: 1ch, *2sc (*UK dc*) into the next sc (*UK dc*), 1sc (*UK dc*) into each of the following 3 sc (*UK dc*)*. Repeat from * to * all around, sl st into the ch at start of round [40 sts].

Rounds 6–12: 1ch, 1sc (*UK dc*) into each sc (*UK dc*), sl st into the ch at start of round.

Round 13: 1ch, *1sc (*UK dc*) into each of the next 3 sc (*UK dc*), skip the following sc (*UK dc*)*. Repeat from * to * all around, sl st into the ch at start of round [30 sts]. At the end of the round, slip some filling into the shape.

Round 14: 1ch, *1sc (*UK dc*) into each of the next 2 sc (*UK dc*), skip the following sc (*UK dc*)*. Repeat from * to * all around, sl st into the ch at start of round [20 sts].

Round 15: 1ch, *1sc (*UK dc*) into the next sc (*UK dc*), skip the following sc (*UK dc*)*. Repeat from * to * all around, sl st into the ch at start of round [10 sts].

Break off the yarn, pass it into the remaining stitches and pull up to close the hole.

Legs (× 4)

Using **A**, 3ch and join with sl st into a ring.

Round 1: 1ch, 8sc (*UK dc*) into the ring, sl st into the ch at start of round [8 sts].

Round 2: change to **C**. 1ch, 2sc (*UK dc*) into each sc (*UK dc*), sl st into the ch at start of round [16 sts].

Rounds 3–6: 1ch, 1sc (*UK dc*) into each sc (*UK dc*), sl st into the ch at start of round. Break off the yarn and slip some filling into the shape.

Muzzle and tummy

Using **A**, 3ch and join with sl st into a ring.

Round 1: 1ch, 8sc (*UK dc*) into the ring, sl st into the ch at start of round [8 sts].

Round 2: 1ch, 2sc (*UK dc*) into each sc (*UK dc*), sl st into the ch at start of round [16 sts]; finish off. Make two of these, one for the muzzle and the other for the tummy.

Ears (× 4)

Using **C**, 4ch and join with sl st into a ring.

Row 1: 1ch, 4sc (*UK dc*) into the ring [4 sts].

Row 2: Turn the work, 1ch, 2sc (*UK dc*) into each sc (*UK dc*) [8 sts].

Row 3: Reverse single crochet (*UK reverse double crochet*) into each sc (*UK dc*); finish off.

ASSEMBLY

Face: Sew the flat edge of each ear on to the top of the head. Sew the muzzle on to the head using backstitch. Using **A**, embroider a French knot for each eye; using **B**, embroider the nose and the mouth using satin stitch.

Joining the parts: Sew the legs on to the front of the body so that the bear is sitting down. Attach the tummy to the middle of the front using backstitch. Join the head to the body.

Snap hook: Join yarn **C** to the top of the head with sl st; 5ch, sl st into the previous stitch, passing through the snap hook, then 5ch and sl st into the head just next to the first stitch. Finish off.

CROCHETED
ANIMAL
CHARMS

34 DONKEY

SIZE: about 6.5cm (2½in) high

MATERIALS

DK (sport) weight yarn (50% wool/50% acrylic): 1 ball each of light grey (**A**) and lime green (**B**)
Embroidery thread/yarn in black and white
Synthetic filling
1 swivel snap hook
1.75mm (US size 6) crochet hook

STITCHES

Foundation chain (ch); slip stitch (sl st); US single crochet/UK double crochet and US reverse single crochet/UK reverse double crochet (see page 64).

INSTRUCTIONS

Head

Using **A**, 3ch and join with sl st into a ring.
Round 1: 1ch, 8sc (*UK dc*) into the ring, sl st into the ch at start of round [8 sts].
Round 2: 1ch, 2sc (*UK dc*) into each sc (*UK dc*), sl st into the ch at start of round [16 sts].
Round 3: 1ch, *2sc (*UK dc*) into the next sc (*UK dc*), 1sc (*UK dc*) into the following sc (*UK dc*)*. Repeat from * to * all around, sl st into the ch at start of round [24 sts].
Rounds 4–9: 1ch, 1sc (*UK dc*) into each sc (*UK dc*), sl st into the ch at start of round.
Round 10: 1ch, *1sc (*UK dc*) into each of the next 3 sc (*UK dc*), skip the following sc (*UK dc*)*. Repeat from * to * all around, sl st into the ch at start of round [18 sts].
Rounds 11–16: 1ch, 1sc (*UK dc*) into each sc (*UK dc*), sl st into the ch at start of round. At the end of round 16, slip some filling into the shape.
Round 17: 1ch, *1sc (*UK dc*) into each of the next 2 sc (*UK dc*), skip the following sc (*UK dc*)*. Repeat from * to * all around, sl st into the ch at start of round [12 sts].
Round 18: 1ch, *1sc (*UK dc*) into the next sc (*UK dc*), skip the following sc (*UK dc*)*. Repeat from * to * all around, sl st into the ch at start of round [6 sts].
Break off the yarn, pass it into the remaining stitches and pull up to close the hole; finish off.

Body

Using **A**, 3ch and join with sl st into a ring.
Round 1: 1ch, 8sc (*UK dc*) into the ring, sl st into the ch at start of round [8 sts].

Round 2: 1ch, 2sc (*UK dc*) into each sc (*UK dc*), sl st into the ch at start of round [16 sts].

Round 3: 1ch, *2sc (*UK dc*) into the next sc (*UK dc*), 1sc (*UK dc*) into the following sc (*UK dc*)*. Repeat from * to * all around, sl st into the ch at start of round [24 sts].

Rounds 4–9: 1ch, 1sc (*UK dc*) into each sc (*UK dc*), sl st into the ch at start of round.

Round 10: 1ch, *1sc (*UK dc*) into each of the next 3 sc (*UK dc*), skip the following sc (*UK dc*)*. Repeat from * to * all around, sl st into the ch at start of round [18 sts]. At the end of the round, slip some filling into the shape.

Round 11: 1ch, *1sc (*UK dc*) into each of the next 2 sc (*UK dc*) skip the following sc (*UK dc*)*. Repeat from * to * all around, sl st into the ch at start of round [12 sts].

Round 12: 1ch, *1sc (*UK dc*) into the next sc (*UK dc*), skip the following sc (*UK dc*)*. Repeat from * to * all around, sl st into the ch at start of round [6 sts].

Break off the yarn, pass it into the remaining stitches and pull up to close the hole; finish off.

Legs (× 4)

Using **A**, 3ch and join with sl st into a ring.

Round 1: 1ch, 8sc (*UK dc*) into the ring, sl st into the ch at start of round [8 sts].

Rounds 2–4: 1ch, 1sc (*UK dc*) into each sc (*UK dc*). Break off the yarn and slip some filling into the shape.

Muzzle

This is worked in an oval shape around a foundation chain. Using **B**, 7ch (includes turning chain).

Round 1: 1sc (*UK dc*) into each of the first 5 ch, 3sc (*UK dc*) into the last ch; then work back down the other side of the foundation chain with 1sc (*UK dc*) into each of the first 5 ch, 2sc (*UK dc*) into the last ch, sl st into the ch at start of row.

Rounds 2–3: 1ch, 1sc (*UK dc*) into each sc (*UK dc*) on this edge, 3sc (*UK dc*) into the centre sc (*UK dc*) of the 3sc (*UK dc*) of the previous round, 1sc (*UK dc*) into each sc (*UK dc*) of the other edge and 2sc (*UK dc*) into the last sc (*UK dc*), sl st into the ch at start of round. Break off the yarn.

Ears (× 2)

The ears are worked in a similar way to the muzzle, around the foundation chain. Using **B**, 16ch (includes turning ch).

Round 1: 14sc (*UK dc*), 5sc (*UK dc*) into the last ch and 14sc (*UK dc*) back up the other side of the chain. Break off the yarn. Using **A**, crochet 1 row of reverse single crochet (*UK reverse double crochet*) all around the ear; finish off.

ASSEMBLY

Face: Sew the muzzle on to the front of the head using backstitch. Embroider the mouth using backstitch in black, the nostrils with satin stitch in black and each eye with a French knot in black with 4 long stitches in white around it.

Legs and ears: Attach the legs. Sew an ear on to each side of the head.

Tail: join yarn **A** to the bottom of the back with sl st, ch10 (includes turning chain). Crochet 1 row of sc (*UK dc*) then join to the back using sl st. Break off the yarn. With a yarn needle, embroider 4 little loops in **A** at the end of the tail.

Snap hook: Join yarn **B** to the top of the head with sl st; 5ch, sl st into the previous stitch, passing through the snap hook, then 5ch and sl st into the head just next to the first stitch. Finish off.

Tip

If you like, you can use plastic safety eyes for the donkey, as you can for all the animals in this section. Just insert them before you stuff the head.

CROCHETED
ANIMAL
CHARMS

35 FROG

SIZE: about 6.5cm (2½in) high

MATERIALS

DK (sport) weight yarn (50% wool/50% acrylic): 1 ball of lime green (**A**)
4-ply (fingering) weight yarn (30% lambswool/70% acrylic): 1 ball of mint green (**B**)
Embroidery yarn in orange
1.75mm (US size 6) crochet hook

STITCHES

Foundation chain (ch), slip stitch (sl st) and US single crochet/UK double crochet (see page 64).

INSTRUCTIONS

Head

Using **B**, 3ch and join with sl st into a ring.

Round 1: 1ch, 8sc (*UK dc*) into the ring, sl st into the ch at start of round [8 sts].

Round 2: 1ch, 2sc (*UK dc*) into each sc (*UK dc*), sl st into the ch at start of round [16 sts].

Round 3: 1ch, *2sc (*UK dc*) into the next sc (*UK dc*), 1sc (*UK dc*) into the following sc (*UK dc*)*. Repeat from * to * all around, sl st into the ch at start of round [24 sts].

Round 4: 1ch, *2sc (*UK dc*) into the next sc (*UK dc*), 1sc (*UK dc*) into each of the following 2 sc (*UK dc*)*. Repeat from * to * all around, sl st into the ch at start of round [32 sts].

Rounds 5–6: 1ch, 1sc (*UK dc*) into each sc (*UK dc*), sl st into the ch at start of round. At the end of round 6, slip some filling into the shape.

Round 7: 1ch, *1sc (*UK dc*) into the next 3 sc (*UK dc*), skip the following sc (*UK dc*)*. Repeat from * to * all around, sl st into the ch at start of round [24 sts].

Round 8: 1ch, *1sc (*UK dc*) into the next 2 sc (*UK dc*), skip the following sc (*UK dc*)*. Repeat from * to * all around, sl st into the ch at start of round [16 sts].

Round 9: 1ch, * 1sc (*UK dc*) into the next sc (*UK dc*), skip the following sc (*UK dc*)*. Repeat from * to * all around, sl st into the ch at start of round [8 sts].

Break off the yarn, pass it into the remaining stitches and pull up to close the hole; finish off.

Body

Using **B**, 3ch and join with sl st into a ring.

Round 1: 1ch, 6sc (*UK dc*) into the ring, sl st into the ch at start of round [6 sts].

Round 2: 1ch, 2sc (*UK dc*) into each sc (*UK dc*), sl st into the ch at start of round [12 sts].

Round 3: 1ch, *2sc (*UK dc*) into the next sc (*UK dc*), 1sc (*UK dc*) into the following 2 sc (*UK dc*)*. Repeat from * to * all around, sl st into the ch at start of round [18 sts].

Rounds 4–10: 1ch, 1sc (*UK dc*) into each sc (*UK dc*), sl st into the ch at start of round. At the end of round 10, slip some filling into the shape.

Round 11: 1ch, *1sc (*UK dc*) into each of the next 2 sc (*UK dc*), skip the following sc (*UK dc*)*. Repeat from * to * all around, sl st into the ch at start round [12 sts].

Round 12: 1ch, *1sc (*UK dc*) into the next sc (*UK dc*), skip the following sc (*UK dc*)*. Repeat from * to * all around, sl st into the ch at start of round [6 sts].

Break off the yarn, pass it into the remaining stitches and pull up to close the hole. Finish off.

Legs (× 2)

Using **B**, 15ch.

Rows 1–2: 1ch, sc (*UK dc*) into each sc (*UK dc*).

Toes: Form four toes at the end of row 2. For each toe, 5ch and sl st into the first ch; finish off.

Arms (× 2)

Using **B**, 9ch.

Rows 1–2: 1ch, sc (*UK dc*) into each sc (*UK dc*).

Fingers: Form four fingers at the end of row 2. For each finger, 5ch and sl st into the first ch; finish off.

Eyes (× 2)

Using **B**, 3ch and join with sl st into a ring.

Round 1: 1ch, 8sc (*UK dc*) into the ring, sl st into the ch at start of round; finish off

Mouth

This is worked in an oval shape around a foundation chain. Using **A**, 8ch (includes turning ch); sc (*UK dc*) into the first 6 ch, 3sc (*UK dc*) into the last ch, then work back down the other side of the foundation chain with 1sc (*UK dc*) into each of the first 6 ch, 2sc (*UK dc*) into the last ch, sl st into the ch at the start; finish off.

ASSEMBLY

Mouth: Attach the mouth to the front of the head using backstitch; separate the lips with a line of backstitch in **B**.

Eyes: Sew the base of the eyes to the top of the head and embroider a French knot in orange in the centre.

Joining the pieces: Attach the legs and the arms to the body. Next attach the head.

Snap hook: Join yarn **B** to the top of the head with sl st; 5ch, sl st into the previous stitch, passing through the snap hook, then 5ch and sl st into the head just next to the first stitch. Finish off.

A big thank you to Auréa Polo and Babette Brouard who
have knitted and crocheted all the cuddly toys in this book,
and to Bruno Verrechia for all the settings.

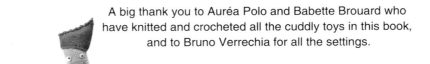

First published in Great Britain 2011 by Search Press Limited,
Wellwood, North Farm Road, Tunbridge Wells, Kent TN2 3DR

Reprinted 2011

Original title: Doudous Animaux: Tricot, Crochet & Tricotin

© 2009 by Editions Marie Claire – Société d'Information et de Créations (SIC)

English translation by Cicero Translations

English edition produced by GreenGate Publishing Services

ISBN: 978-1-84448-607-6